This Can't Be Normal

Diana Estill

Author of the *Driving on the Wrong Side of the Road*

First Print Edition: March 2013
ISBN 13: 978-0-9799708-9-4
ISBN 10: 0-9799708-9-X

Corcob Press, an imprint of Totally Skewed Productions
120 E. FM 544, Ste. 72, PMB 135
Murphy, TX, 75094

Cover and Formatting: Streetlight Graphics

For information, contact Diana Estill, Totally Skewed Productions, TotallySkewed.com.

TABLE OF CONTENTS

GARAGE SALE MAMA

M Y MOTHER AND I HAD little in common when it came to shopping preferences. While I loved going to malls and using coupons, Mom most enjoyed finding a good garage sale. She'd been that way ever since I was a child.

Mom simply couldn't wait for the next chance to spend a few dollars on someone else's discards. And it made her even happier to turn around and give those found "treasures" to her children. Thus, none of us offspring ever knew what we'd receive from her for Christmas. Whatever the gift, we could be sure it would be ill-conceived, somewhat strange, and entirely entertaining.

One year, right after my husband and I had married and moved into a contemporary house filled with southwestern décor, Mom gave me a wooden goose paper towel holder. Now, this was not a small goose. The fairytale-inspired image stood as high as the towels it had been designed to hide.

To enhance this decorative piece of counter clutter, Mom had painted the words "Diana's Kitchen" on the goose. I presume she wanted me to lay claim to the room that nobody, especially my husband and teenage children, had ever threatened to command.

That whole country kitchen look had gone out of style about a decade earlier. Mom had been among the last to realize this—or to care. Had I set this aquatic replica on my Mexican-tile countertop, it would have appeared no less inharmonious than a Geisha statue.

Looking back, I now realize that the Mother Goose paper towel holder was actually one of the most functional presents Mom ever had given me. That gift was followed by a hideous teacup and saucer, from which a small cat figure peeked at me through fur that appeared to have been skinned from a *real* feline! Probably the pelts were rabbit, but that didn't do much to reduce the "ick" factor.

The next year, Mom didn't have to mail her gifts because she visited us for Christmas. She was dismayed when she didn't see the goose paper towel holder. I didn't lie when I told my mother we'd used but no longer had the kitchen apparatus. I figured it best not to disclose that we'd used the holder for firewood. Hey, don't judge me. It had been a cold night, and we'd run out of logs.

I felt terrible about having burned up Mom's gift. She'd gone to all the trouble to paint my name on it, and I'd incinerated her handiwork. Whatever she'd brought to give me that year would have to be prominently displayed. That would be my penance, I decided.

"We have to act like we love whatever Mom gives us," I said to my husband.

"Okay, but what does that mean?" he asked.

"No matter what it is, we've got to set it where she can see we're using it."

Imagine our surprise when, on Christmas Eve, we opened a life-sized portrait of a wild buck deer. The photo was mounted in rough cedar, so the frame had possibilities. But the giant deer head with the hyper-alert gaze belonged in a hunting cabin...or more appropriately, at a shooting range.

"Wow!" I said when I peeled off the wrapping paper.

"That's really nice," my husband cooed in a voice I'd never before heard from him.

"I thought you could hang it in your living room," Mom offered proudly.

Our living room, which included adobe-inspired furnishings, hand-woven Mayan rugs, and native Indian pottery, would so be complemented by this new addition.

The next day, in the wee hours of Christmas morning, Hubby woke me up. "Come in here," he said. "I have something to show you."

I tried to guess at his motive. Maybe he had a special surprise for me, something he wanted to give me in private before the kids awakened. Possibly he'd bought me some naughty nightie he didn't want Mom to see. He put a finger to his lips, motioning for me to follow. Together, we padded down the hallway toward the living room where the Christmas tree stood in all its splendor. My spouse checked the stairway as we passed, to see if anyone might be nearby. I glanced at the fireplace as we entered the main room where the festivities would soon unfold. The stockings hung undisturbed.

Hubby tugged my hand and led me to a wall next to the bar area. I'd last stood there days earlier, while hanging a professional Christmas photo of

5

our two granddaughters. I'd had the picture made that season, and the girls, then ages 2 and 5, had worn matching outfits that I'd sewn for them. That beautifully framed, 21- by 16-inch portrait was among my prized possessions. I glimpsed where I'd last seen that keepsake. Staring back at me was a horned game animal.

My mouth fell open. And then I burst out laughing. I'd never seen anything funnier in my entire life. Perhaps it was the early hour, or maybe the shock of expecting to see one thing and then finding something completely different that did it. The harder I struggled to control my guffaws, the more difficult it was for my prankster to restrain himself.

Before we knew it, we'd awakened Mom. I heard her footsteps on the stairs and fought to regain composure.

"What's so funny?" Mom asked, entering the living room.

"Oh, he was just showing me how that deer's eyes can follow you," I said.

Mom studied the photo. "Huh."

Behind Mom's back, I gave Hubby a look that dared him to say anything.

For the next few days, until Mom left, we lived in harmony with that wildlife target adorning our wall. A few months later, we sold the deer photo in a garage sale.

I failed to ask the purchaser if she needed a gift receipt.

<hr>

I wasn't the only beneficiary of Mom's thrift

purchases. My husband once opened a present from her that contained a toy pool table about the size of a half-sheet of paper. The game was missing all the balls and one cue stick.

That same year, I received a paint-by-number kit. Had I completed the craft, I would have wound up with an eight-by-ten image of a palomino horse's head.

"I know you like horses," Mom explained by phone.

I didn't bother to remind her I'd done so as a teenager. Instead, I simply thanked her and gave the paint-by-number kit to one of my grandchildren.

My oldest son, Ron, who works in law enforcement, once received a talking cop cookie jar from Mom. Every time its hat-shaped lid opened, the policeman screamed, "Step away from the cookie jar!" We spent an entire evening playing with that amusing gift.

PHOTO ABOVE: Ron attempts to mimic cookie jar cop's expression.

Not to be slighted, my daughter-in-law Julie, who's an educator, took the prize one year for best teacher. No kidding. Mom sent her a gift set that included shower lotion, body gel, and body mist labeled "Greatest Teacher." None of the products' stickers hinted at their fragrance.

Julie examined the bath set and said, "I can see myself wearing this to school and someone asking, 'What's that scent you're wearing?'" She laughed. "I guess I'd have to tell them, 'It's *Greatest Teacher!*'"

It's not that the family wasn't appreciative of Mom's offerings, confusing as they often were. We were happy to know she thought enough of us to want to bestow presents on us. But we'd have been equally enthused if she'd sent a card and saved her money. Many times, I tried to get her to do so before I realized that her gift selections didn't stem from frivolous choices or a lack of funds. They were about Mom's thrill of the hunt (perhaps literally, given that deer picture) and her limited closet space.

Mom eventually admitted to me that she visited garage and estate sales year-round as her primary form of entertainment. She had a closet in which she kept everything she bought for future gifts. Once a year, she emptied that storage, put sticky notes on all the items to identify the recipients, and shipped the presents. By clearing her closet, she regained sufficient room to support another year of garage sale visits.

I can't be too critical, as I've been known to exhibit similar behavior. Only when I do that, I call it "donating to charity."

The items Mom sent to others had more to do

with what she thought was a good buy than what she expected anyone to like.

"She gave me a toy car!" my brother once exclaimed during a comparison match.

"Oh, that's nothing," I replied. "I got a talking George Bush doll!"

Mom's gifts were always good for White Elephant parties and re-gifting because she had an innate talent for unearthing weird stuff.

"Where did you find that George Bush doll?" I asked her.

With no hint of reservation, she offered, "At a truck stop."

At least I knew the origins of the presidential likeness. I couldn't say the same for the bath set she'd given me the previous year. The football-shaped tin displayed a small bottle of shower gel, a jar of "body soufflé," and a gingerbread-man-shaped soap bar. The whole kit suggested ingestible qualities. The shower gel was labeled Gingerbread Latte. But even I knew better than to drink it.

A large sticker affixed to the back of the metal container cautioned me to "Use only as directed," and "Do not apply around eyes or lips." That ruled out washing my face with those products, but I kept reading. "Excessive use or prolonged exposure may cause irritation to skin and urinary tract."

Was this a bath set or antibiotics? I decided to refrain from using any of it. In fact, I didn't even want to chance opening the shrink-wrapped container indoors. I don't know where Mom had found those hazardous materials. Given the warning label, I'd say that bath set might have been manufactured in Fukushima.

While visiting Mom in Florida one November, I ventured with her to a nearby consignment store. The word "consignment" can be defined in different ways, depending on region. In my mother's area, consignment stores offer what look like remains from multi-family garage sales—old shoes, rusted tools, outdated books, trinkets, and costume jewelry last worn during the Carter administration. But to Mom, a flea market was more exciting than New York's famed Fifth Avenue.

Mom's eyes brightened as she reached to retrieve a Santa Claus doll seated on a miniature motorcycle. Scanning the ornament (if you can call something that looks like a substitute for a singing Billy Bass plaque an ornament), she found a button. She punched it, and the Santa came to life, singing Elvis's *Blue Christmas.* The Santa figure stood up and swiveled his hips as he lip-synced to The King's music.

"Oh, loooook," Mom said. With childlike fascination, she held the gadget as I searched for a place to escape. "I had one just like this once," she confessed. "But I gave it away." She frowned. "I should have kept it."

"Who'd you give it to?" I couldn't recall any family members having complained about a singing Santa.

"Someone at the hospital." Mom pushed the button again. "I wonder if Kerry would want this for Christmas."

I felt it was my big-sisterly duty to spare my brother from this abomination, so I did the only reasonable thing. I bought the Santa for Mom.

At last, I'd figured out the mystery behind her

holiday purchases. The gifts she sent weren't random discount buys. They were items she truly wanted for herself but couldn't justify owning. Maybe that resulted from a lack of self-esteem—or possibly a shortage of closets.

Back at Mom's house, she proudly set the Santa on top of her TV. Then she turned and asked, "You want to see my fireplace?"

Mom didn't have a fireplace, so I said yes and waited for what would unfold. She pulled out a DVD and slipped it into the player. Instantly, her television screen displayed an image of a hearth, complete with the sounds of crackling cinders.

"That's nice," I remarked. "Where'd you get it?" The DVD didn't seem like something Mom would have turned up at a garage sale.

"Off *QVC*."

Suddenly, I recalled Kerry's house didn't have a fireplace, either. "You know," I said, "maybe Kerry would like *that* for Christmas." If she couldn't find something suitable for my brother, I thought I'd drop some hints.

"Yeah? You think so?"

"Sure."

I never thought another moment about that video until the following month.

A few days after Christmas, I received an email message from Kerry. "Can you believe what Mom sent me for Christmas this year? A fireplace video!" He wasn't enamored with the gift.

Apparently, Mom hadn't needed my help as much as I'd thought.

By Mom's final year of life, I'd learned to appreciate her quirky tastes and her generosity. Earlier, I'd been perplexed and maybe even somewhat hurt by her gift selections. It seemed she knew little about me. And I felt equally clueless about her.

Shortly before Mom died, my stepdad told me, "When I met your mother, I told her my house was her house. She could do whatever she wanted with it." He grinned. "And she filled it *up!*"

Indeed she had.

And if she'd had her way, she'd have filled up mine too.

This will be my first Christmas without my mother and her humorous gifts. I will miss the anticipation of what might arrive.

Do you suppose there are garage sales in heaven?

DYING TO BE SEEN

FOR SOCIAL CONTACT AND THE promise of cake, some people get a kick out of birthday parties. My father, on the other hand, prefers funerals.

It's not that Dad wants anyone to die, necessarily. He just enjoys a chance to catch up with old friends, even if he's sometimes a bit late in doing so, as in, they've already kicked the bucket.

"I had to go to a classmate's funeral today," Dad said over the phone. With a hint of gloom, he added, "I went to the viewing last night."

I couldn't think of anyone he had kept in touch with from high school. And the weather on the previous night had been nothing short of horrid. "Whose was it?" I asked, thinking someone who'd been extremely close to my father had died.

Dad uttered a man's name I'd never heard.

"How long has it been since you last saw him?" I asked.

"I went to *school* with him," Dad said.

"So that was the last time you'd seen him?"

"Until today, yes." He sounded annoyed.

"I don't get it." I did the math. "That was over fifty years ago. Why would you bother to attend the viewing *and* funeral of someone you haven't worried about seeing *alive* for over fifty years?"

"Because everyone I went to school with was going to be there!"

See, that's how my father thinks. This wasn't so much about his grief over the loss of a classmate as it was a potential high school reunion.

When family members become ill, my siblings and I don't tell Dad if we can help it. At the first sign of sickness, he starts searching for a good obit photo. Okay, that might be an exaggeration, but he does take his dark suit to the cleaners.

Once, my father called to ask if I could download some music for him. He owns two computers, but he refuses to purchase anything that requires him to use a credit card online. Others might steal his identity—and then *they'd* begin receiving all the funeral notices, I suppose.

"What song do you want?" I waited to hear him mention some obscure title by an artist who'd previously departed. Most of the music Dad enjoys predates the digital age.

"*Danny Boy.*"

"*Danny Boy*? There must be thousands of recordings of that song, Dad. Which one do you want?"

"Oh, at least three different ones would be good, so long as they sound traditional. It's for Dorothy."

Dorothy is my great aunt, and I didn't know whether she had a computer. What I did understand was that this whole exercise was going to involve me downloading some songs, burning them to CDs, and driving to Dad's house (10 miles from mine), so he could in turn drive another 15 miles to Dorothy's house to deliver the songs she wanted. But hey, what are daughters for?

"Why does she want several versions of the song *Danny Boy*?"

"She asked me to plan the music for her funeral," Dad offered in a tone that suggested I should have already known that. "And she's Irish and wants to use that song."

Good grief! I had no idea my aunt was near death. In fact, Dad had failed to even mention she'd been sick. "What happened?"

"Huh? Nothing happened," Dad said. "I just need her to tell me which version she likes so I'll have it when the time comes."

"Isn't that something the church would normally handle?"

"She doesn't want it played during the *church* service. She wants it played at the graveside. And she asked me to see to it."

I envisioned my father standing in a cemetery, holding a boom box wailing bagpipe music and the lyrics to *Danny Boy*. I could definitely see how that would be a mood enhancer.

That conversation took place more than four years ago. Aunt Dorothy passed away a few months back. By the time *Danny Boy* was needed, possibly Dad had forgotten where he put that CD. But somebody surfaced with a copy, and at Dorothy's wishes, the Irish were well represented at her graveside service.

Funeral opportunities continue for Dad because, when you're nearly 80 years old, there's rarely a week that goes by that a cousin to your father's barber's wife's sister doesn't keel over. Circle of life and all that.

My father reports his funeral attendances as

though he's building mileage points toward a world cruise. And this frequently leaves me at a loss for words. What can I say to a man whose social coordinator is an undertaker? I keep in touch with friends via email and Facebook. Dad networks through the obituaries.

At 7:55 a.m. one Monday morning, Dad called to give me his itinerary. "I'll be at a funeral today."

I've no idea why he tells me these things because I know that anytime I can't reach him, he's either in a funeral service or out taking his dark suit to the cleaners. I stirred the grits I'd been cooking and punched the timer on the microwave while I waited for him to reveal who'd sponsored that day's social gathering.

"Do you remember that woman that Mama used to be good friends with? Ms. Carter?"

I recalled my deceased grandmother's associate as a petite, quiet woman who attended church regularly. Unless memory failed me, she'd have been over 100 years old by then, and I was fairly certain she'd gone to meet her maker some time ago.

"Elizabeth?"

"Yes," Dad confirmed.

"Didn't she die a while back?"

"Yeah, but her son married that other woman that used to be Mama's best friend." Dad paused a moment. "Ms. Reynolds. Remember?"

Ms. Reynolds had died some twenty years before my grandmother, so I had no idea where this explanation was leading. It was too early in the morning for me to play a genealogical game of connect-the-branches. "Yes, I remember her," I said, knowing if I'd denied it, I'd be opening the door for a lengthier line of questioning that would cause me to overcook my breakfast.

"Well, their two kids married. And the husband...I can't remember his name...just died of prostate cancer." Dad let out a heavy sigh. "I missed the viewing last night because nobody told me about his death in time for me to go."

I tried to think of something to say to console my grieving father. Then I wondered which part of his story most warranted that effort. Not yet fully alert at that early morning hour, I was also mentally preoccupied with a mean hay fever episode I'd been battling for two days. However, I didn't dare mention my illness to Dad. What would have been the point? His dark suit was already clean.

DRIVING EACH OTHER CRAZY

OST COUPLES DISAGREE ON WHAT constitutes good driving. That's probably due to physical reflexes. Much like other aspects of marriage, when it comes to driving, individual response times differ. Thus, when a passenger notices brake lights ahead, the driver's reaction may not be in sync with the passenger's expectations, resulting in the car still traveling at an unimpeded speed while the person riding shotgun is silently rehearsing the Lord's Prayer.

For this reason, I suggest that if a couple must travel together in the same vehicle, it is advisable that one occupant—preferably the one who isn't behind the steering wheel—wear a blindfold. Failing that, the non-driver should consider riding in the trunk. Nothing else I've tried has been effective at reducing arguments.

"Shouldn't you be in the right lane?" I'll say to my husband. It's not a question, really. More like a criticism. That's abbreviated code for, "If you were paying *any* attention to where you're going, you would know that you have to make a right turn within the next thirty seconds, and you would note that there is currently a steady stream of autos driven by others who *are* cognizant of their whereabouts and have so prepared by already being in the correct lane, which means that those motorists are not about to let you squeeze in at the last minute when you wake up and realize where you are."

But that first comment just sounds so much more congenial. And it takes a lot less breath.

Hubby's response is always the same. He'll stare straight ahead, possibly still mentally evaluating yesterday's football game or whatever else is responsible for his preoccupation, and reply, "Eventually."

This verbal exchange is regularly followed by him shouting, "You sonofa...! Why won't you let me over?"

The problem occurs repeatedly because my spouse prefers to drive in the middle lane. His theory goes like this: if he is in the center lane, then he has to cross only one lane to be in the correct turn position. But if he's in the far left or right lane, and he suddenly sees something on the opposite side of the road that strikes his fancy (or he abruptly remembers his locale), then he might not be able to cross two lanes fast enough to circumvent an increase in auto insurance premiums.

I, on the other hand, begin planning my turns as soon as I pull out of the garage. If I need to make a left in three miles, I'll start off driving in the left lane as soon as I leave my house. I might even switch on a turn signal when I start the engine. Okay, maybe not that soon. But I do use turn signals 100 percent of the time, and that includes when I'm exiting the driveway. It's just good form developed when I was a student driver, back before I became my spouse's instructor.

Still, I don't always act like an adult when I'm behind the wheel. That's especially true when Hubby and I are arguing. Proof of that occurred on a trip many years ago when we were traveling west of Houston.

In the middle of some gripe session for which I cannot recall the trigger nor the topic, my husband said, "Just pull over right now and let me out of here."

So I did.

I braked from 70 mph to a stop on the shoulder of some highway I'd never before driven, and he opened the passenger door and got out of the minivan. I know. I'm not proud of that. It's hard to admit I ever drove that style vehicle. Anyway, having a full head of steam, I decided I'd turn this into a teachable moment. For him, that is.

After he slammed the door, I drove off and left him standing on the side of the highway. *Ha! I bet he never expected me to do that! I'll drive over that hill so he won't see me before I turn around.*

Unbeknownst to me, it was several more miles to the nearest exit. And even after I'd turned around, I had to travel a long distance in the opposite direction before I could make another U-turn and retrieve my disgruntled passenger. *What if he thumbs a ride with a trucker, gets picked off by some nut case, and I have to explain my way out of a murder rap?*

It wasn't funny then, but we laugh about it today—just as we do about the time he deserted me and the kids in Disney World. In a fit, he left the four of us in a hot minivan and stormed off across the vast parking lot, taking the car keys with him.

Now, if you've ever been to Disney World, you know

how large those parking lots are and how difficult it would be to find anyone who'd wandered away in one—especially before the invention of cellphones. And if you haven't ever visited "The Happiest Place on Earth" (which, by the way, is a huge misnomer), then imagine an Ikea store parking lot on steroids, and you'll conjure the right image.

I didn't even try to hunt the man down, as I wasn't about to go off and leave our children in the car alone. The only thing I knew to do was wait him out. Soon he'd remember that all our money and credit cards were in my purse.

That recognition must have flashed quickly because he came right back and apologized. He explained he'd been set off by the constant quibbling among our brood. The children had been going at each other for two straight days, and he'd simply reached his fill of their complaints.

As he climbed inside the van and cranked the engine, one of the girls looked longingly at him and said, "Hurry up and turn on the air. We're *hot*."

Nowadays, we seldom have these distressing episodes. The children are all grown, and we've each lost hope of ever conforming to the other's driving standards. Our rolling quarrels now center more on maps.

On a recent trip we made with another couple, I claimed the driver's seat. The other gal traveling with us had said she struggled with car sickness. Because we were winding through the Texas Hill Country, we thought it best to let her ride in the front passenger seat and have the two men sit together in the rear of the sedan. Women up front, men in back, just the way God intended it, you know.

I handed Hubby the map and asked him to direct me to Utopia, a remote town few had ever heard of before Robert Duvall made it famous in the movie *Seven Days in Utopia.* Hollywood doesn't know when to leave a sleepy town in its slumber. Thanks to this area's newfound stardom, we were all in serious danger of missing lunch.

But I'm getting ahead of myself.

Before we could find grub, we first had to find a city. When you're driving through parts of the Texas Hill Country, it's easier to spot wild turkey (the kind that gobble, not the kind you drink) than it is to find a restaurant. I knew of one diner in Utopia that held promise: Lost Maples Café, a down-home-cooking place that had been featured in *Seven Days in Utopia.* This joint made pies that tasted so good they often distracted hunters from shooting deer. Like the little tin tabletop signs inside claimed, "Pie fixes everything." Right then, I hoped it could cure motion sickness.

"This road doesn't go through to Utopia," Hubby crooned from the back seat.

"Yes, it does," I said. Having looked at the course before I'd relinquished the map to my directionally challenged mate, I knew I'd seen a pin dot identified as Utopia on that folded paper. If there had been any cell coverage in that primitive area, I could have proven so with my smart phone.

"No. I'm looking at the map, and Utopia isn't even on here."

My passenger-seat friend clutched her stomach as I turned the car around and headed back in the direction we'd previously driven. About 10 miles later, after I'd wound through a series of hairpin curves and steep grades, praying we wouldn't soon need a barf bag for the woman next to me, Mr. GPS piped up and said, "Oh, wait a minute. I see it on here, now. You were going the right way the first time."

I didn't put him out on the side of the road. But that doesn't mean that I didn't briefly consider it.

BLENDER WARS

MY SON RON BOUGHT A blender. Not just any blender, mind you, but one of those gizmos that can double as a wood chipper. Being an "early adopter," Ron had been first to own the most current cellphone, computer, and TV. And Hubby had reacted to each purchase as if it had signaled a throwdown. He prided himself on being a latecomer who won by waiting—which, come to think of it, is how he married me.

My spouse enjoyed taunting our son about his buying habits. Within a few months of Ron's latest acquisition, Hubby would claim to have located either a better price or a superior product. Back and forth it would go until one of them upgraded or moved on to the next gadget, at which point the cycle would start all over again. Their behaviors were almost as exhausting to witness as they were to finance.

After he'd been introduced to Ron's new kitchen appliance, my tech-obsessed mate researched blenders like a smoothie storeowner with an impulse-control disorder. Finally, he settled on a product he thought would turn him into the world's best shake master. He ordered the contraption online and waited for the chance to announce his purchase to Ron.

When we next visited my son's house, Ron bragged to his competitor, "My blender can make peanut butter from raw peanuts. I bet yours can't do *that.*"

"Yes, it can," Hubby scoffed. "And mine also came with a wide-mouth jar."

Both men were intrigued by the flavors their appliances could not only create but also disguise. The shake, soup, and ice cream recipes listed inside the accompanying owner manuals encouraged the addition of raw greens in everything from breakfast beverages to desserts. *Throw it all in here*, these blenders begged. *We can pulverize whatever you give us! Floral arrangements? No problem. Avocado seeds? Wine corks? Who wants extra fiber?*

Aside from the price tag, the problem with my spouse's new find was that it operated at the same decibel level as a front-end loader. Every morning before work, he mixed his liquid breakfast. I don't know what was in those drinks, but the blender noise suggested at least a bushel of acorns.

Rhe, rhe, rhe, rhe, Rhe, Rhe, Rhe, Rhe, RHEEEEEE, RHEEEEEE, RHEEEEEE, RHEEEEEE, RHEEEEEE, RHEEEEEE, RHEEEEEE, the obnoxious machine screamed as it churned. (Actually, I *condensed* that quote to save reading time.) The motor ran so long that it had a countdown at the end of its program to show how many seconds remained until the beast would be silenced. This, no doubt, dramatically reduced occurrences of suicide.

"Good grief!" I shouted from bed. "What are you making that requires so much processing?"

"Just a smoothie," Hubby hollered back. "It has to go through the full cycle."

Unlike me, my husband loved hearing the blender activate so much that he would stand inches from it any time he switched on the device. "It has a powerful motor," he explained. "That's why it makes so much noise." He stood fixated as though watching the mechanical process of crushing ice and frozen fruit was better than attending a high-rise demolition. The blender, nonetheless, was more likely to produce the need for earplugs.

I don't understand why guys get all giddy over thunderous grinding sounds. The words "loud" and "powerful" are not necessarily synonymous. Case in point: my neighbor's beagle.

My guy is enamored with ignition switches (except the ones on vacuum cleaners) and "pulse" buttons. Presumably this attraction is related to his affinity for explosions. I guess blending at high speeds is similar to a detonation, though one requires far less cleanup.

Personally, I liked blenders better before they became tools of male fascination on par with the potato gun. What once was a predominately female concern has somehow morphed into a symbol of manhood.

Women, however, are better suited than men for selecting small kitchen appliances because we know which benefits are most important. We check capacity levels to see how many quarts a food processor will hold. (Yeah, we're kind of programmed that way.) We don't ask about rpm (Reverberations Prove Manliness) levels or horsepower because we don't plan to pull or haul anything with a blender.

Ladies mostly want to know if a kitchen device

will break easily, if it can be cleaned without fear of amputation, and most importantly, if it's earned the approval of Bobby Flay. We don't ask how fast a blender will run or if it's capable of turning lumber into sawdust. It's a drink maker, not a food disposal. Though, given what some individuals mix with them, I'll admit that's not always an easy distinction.

My daughter-in-law decided to experiment with Ron's state-of-the-art equipment by making chocolate ice cream inside his prized juicer. I witnessed the contents: Nestle Quick mix, one whole date (pitted), liquid coffee creamer, part of an avocado, and some spinach leaves.

As the blender whirred and my skeptical mate looked on, I mentally compared that device to the contraption we owned. Ron's appliance was quieter, even after allowing for the date pit his wife had neglected to remove.

Score one round for Ron.

The ice cream concoction looked delicious, despite its odd ingredients. I tasted the dessert. "This is excellent!"

My daughter-in-law scrawled the recipe on a notecard. "Here," she offered. "You might want to make it sometime."

"How many calories are in a serving?" I asked.

She shrugged.

Diet food this wasn't. But watching the blender churn all those unlikely combinations into an appealing treat had been worthy entertainment.

Hubby's face registered defeat.

At home, Mr. I-Will-Not-Be-Outdone had to prove our machine hadn't been bested. "I'm going to make that ice cream in *my* blender," he declared.

I watched as he tossed enough greens to make a large salad into the device. "Are you sure we need that much spinach?" I asked.

Hubby squinted and looked at the recipe card. "Yep, it says two cups." He blended the ice cream and then gave me a bowl filled with what looked like frozen baby poop.

I studied the disaster and made a face. Then I scooped a teaspoonful of his creation into my mouth. It tasted like chocolate spinach with a mild fruitiness and a hint of Bermuda grass.

"It's *not* the blender," Hubby insisted. "She gave us the wrong proportions."

Obviously, he'd gone overboard on the spinach. A quarter cup would have come closer to delivering the kind of ice cream we'd shared at Ron's house. Perhaps the recipe had been inadvertently miswritten. But then again, some folks will go to any extreme to prove a point.

"You know, Ron really *does* have the better blender," I said.

My funny guy smirked. "Yeah? Well, he paid a hundred dollars *more* for his."

CAT CRAP COFFEE

F IRST, IT WAS A BLENDER, then a coffeemaker, and finally a coffee grinder. Give a man an inch, and he'll take your whole countertop. And he'll hemorrhage money like he's an oil sheik while doing it.

After my husband bought the blender my son had goaded him into acquiring, he started exploring coffeemakers. The Mr. Coffee machine we'd owned for ten years had recently lost its perk. So we'd borrowed a coffeemaker from another couple with whom we're friends.

"Wow! So this is their *extra* one?" Hubby marveled. "What do they use every day?"

"They've got a one-cup thingy that you have to buy special packets for," I replied. "I don't get it, either. Why would anyone pay two hundred dollars for a coffeepot that'll only make *one* cup at a time?"

He looked at me as though I'd just asked why humans copulate. "Because it makes better-tasting coffee."

I wouldn't have known that because I get my caffeine through sodas. While I love the smell of coffee, I can't stand the flavor unless the brew is first frozen, diluted with whipping cream, dusted with sugar, sprinkled with cinnamon, and topped with a cherry. I also prefer not to make my own drinks. It's simply more fun when I'm not the one who's responsible for cleanup.

My spouse, on the other hand, enjoys grinding his own beans, brewing his own coffee, and leaving behind the remains. So I was nonplussed when he decided to buy a $300 coffeemaker that doesn't use disposable filters. This behemoth had a tower and docking station for the pot, and it took up two feet of counter space that could have been otherwise used for...well ideally, nothing.

I hate counter clutter. But no one who's ever visited our house would guess that.

After Hubby purchased the new coffeemaker, he decided it was time to upgrade the grinder. He'd pushed the former one past its limits for so long that the motor had given out.

"I'll get you another coffee grinder when I go to the mall," I offered.

"No, thank you. I already found the one I want online."

"How much is it?"

"You don't want to know."

I'd asked the wrong question. Had I been smart, I would have inquired about *size* instead of price. But like most gals, I've been previously trained to disregard dimensions.

The new coffee grinder was almost as tall as the java maker, and it could effectively compete with the blender for the title of World's Most Irritating Sound. Despite all the irksome kitchen noises, Gadget Guy insisted he'd achieved the consummate coffee flavor. He could, if he chose, become a full-fledged barista!

Considering Hubby's fascination with the perfect cup of joe, I was intrigued when I read about the most expensive brew in the world: cat poop coffee. (I'm not making this up.) Otherwise known as Kopi Luwak in Indonesia, this product is made from rare coffee beans found in civet (a cat-like creature that resembles a raccoon) feces.

What begins as coffee cherries is consumed by the civets and then as the beans pass through the digestive tracts, they remain intact but are fermented (sort of like pintos passing through people). The beans are picked from the dung, dried in the sun, roasted, and sold to people who have no sense of smell and can't read ingredient labels. At least, that's the only explanation I can offer for why anyone would drink such a beverage.

According to a *New York Times* article, Kopi Luwak is a brew that is "smooth, chocolaty, and devoid of any bitter aftertaste."

*After*taste? Who cares about the aftertaste? What about the primary flavor? Telling me this coffee is smooth and chocolaty doesn't reveal much. I could achieve that description by sticking a Tootsie Roll in a cup of steaming sewage.

Several sources have cited the brew's "distinctive odor." Sounds like marketing code for "putrid stench" to me. Yeah, I'd think it might smell a bit like...oh, I don't know, maybe a civet's ass.

Imagine how hard it could be to find participants for a blind taste test.

Researcher: "Excuse me, miss. Do you drink coffee?"

Potential Taster: "Yes."
Researcher: "Are you able to smell aromas?"
Potential Taster: "Yes."
Researcher: "Okay. Thank you for your time."

At first, I thought this whole idea of cat poop coffee was a farce. Surely nobody was selling civet crap coffee beans here in America. A quick Internet check proved me wrong. One vendor's website suggested the coffee would make "a perfect gift for Dad." Uh, okay, perhaps if you're passive-aggressive and seeking revenge for a rotten childhood. Elsewise, I think if Daddy-O received such a gift, he might boot you out of his basement or strike you from his will.

Reading about this novelty product caused me to contemplate my cat and what hidden treasures might be lurking in her litter box. Sometimes she does eat corn. Would it ferment in her belly? Maybe I could establish a market for cat poop whiskey!

But I nixed that idea when I realized how difficult it would be to hire poop pickers. It's hard enough to locate a man to mow my lawn. Then there was that whole liquor license requirement, and given government red tape, I figured I'd lose interest before I had made it halfway through the application form.

Curious about civets and their natural environment, I Google searched the mammal. One article I found said civets not only eat coffee cherries but also prey on *rodents*!

How about some rat hair with that latte?

I couldn't wait to tell my husband he'd never have a cup of the most revered coffee in the world unless he was willing to buy beans plucked from dung instead of trees. It would be a beautiful moment. I could just imagine the look on his face when I described the origins of this rare beverage.

When Hubby arrived home from work, I said, "I found a new coffee for you to try!"

He flashed a smile. "You did? What is it?" He appeared pleased that I'd thought of him and his fondness for a good morning blend. Most of the time, I ignore (or write about) his coffee habits.

"It's called 'cat poop coffee.'" I giggled. "And it's considered a delicacy."

"It's made from cat turds?"

"Sort of. It's made from coffee beans that have been eaten and pooped from something called a civet, a cat-like animal." I studied him for a reaction, but he showed none. "It's selling here in the U.S. for hundreds of dollars per pound."

His eyebrows arched with interest. "Does it come in decaf?"

AN IMPORTANT SAFETY ADVISORY

T HANKS TO A NASTY BOUT of product recalls, I can now add food phobia to my list of afflictions. The risk of consuming tainted edibles has made me so paranoid that I'm checking the serial numbers and dates on everything in my pantry. Not only did I toss out the peanut butter encased in a jar displaying the product code 2111, but I also kept searching to be sure nothing on my shelves had been stamped with the numbers 666.

When I first heard about the salmonella link to peanut butter, I considered the standard ingredients: peanuts, peanut oil, salt, sugar. Not a single salmon or fish-based product in there anywhere. How, I wondered, could a nutty-flavored sandwich spread become contaminated?

I turned to the Centers for Disease Control and Prevention to learn more about salmonella, and that's when the situation grew more alarming. According to the CDC website, "Salmonella has been known to cause illness for over 100 years." This is appalling! That's way too long for anyone to be sick!

Reading on, I discovered that salmonella, a group of bacteria, live in animal and bird...uh, well, I should remain professional and use the proper word for this, but then some of you might be disappointed, so I'll rely on the more familiar vernacular: *doo-doo*.

This begs the question: who's been pooping in my peanut butter? I knew mice could be attracted to traps baited with peanut butter, but I didn't want to explore that idea any further because it's just too gross. However, I have a morbid curiosity, so I conducted a little more research. I learned that the FDA permits up to 30 insect fragments and one rat hair per 100 grams of peanut butter. (For reference, there are 510 grams of peanut butter in a standard 18-ounce jar.) This level of contamination is considered "aesthetic." *Aesthetic*? Good grief, do we not pay enough tax dollars to buy this agency a dictionary?

But here's the most upsetting part of this latest (assuming another one isn't announced before I finish this copy) grocery product recall: Peanut butter has always been my fallback food. It's been my one sure safety meal in the event of an emergency, like a power outage, famine, or unexpected visit from the grandkids.

When I was young, my father repeatedly told me, "You can live a long time on just peanut butter."

I'm not sure why he shared that with me. It might have been less a statement about survival tactics than insight into his views on Mom's cooking. Nonetheless, I accepted his message as fact. Consequently, I once smuggled a jar of peanut butter (an illegal import, but at the time I didn't know it) into Mexico. No one confiscated my stash, which meant I escaped both discovery and the "Mexican Riviera Runs." Though I must admit peanut butter on tortillas isn't quite the same as a PB&J sandwich.

It distresses me now to learn that my stand-by safety spread has come into question. If the quality of a food as innocuous as peanut butter cannot be insured, then how can I feel protected when buying yogurt? I don't eat yogurt. But that's beside the point.

That new blender my husband bought is going to come in handy in the future, I guess. From now on, we'll make our own peanut butter from raw peanuts. And at my house, we won't allow *any* insect fragments or rat hairs per 100 grams of product. Unfortunately, I can't guarantee my homemade version will be free of *my* hair.

Though the recent food recalls have been discouraging, the related announcements are equally alarming. In a news release, the FDA provided the following statement:

"The Food and Drug Administration (FDA) is warning consumers not to eat certain jars of...<brand name deleted to protect my personal assets> peanut butter or...<private label brand deleted to protect my joint assets> peanut butter due to risk of contamination with *Salmonella* Tennessee, a bacterium that causes food-borne illness."

Here's an addendum to that advisory, this one from me:

Regardless of contents or their state of origin, it is *always* unwise to eat *jars*.

In a follow-up announcement, the CDC recommended that persons in possession of certain brands of peanut butter with containers marked with the product code 2111 should "discard the jar." It's possible that compliance would not only prevent an individual from consuming the container but would also reduce the manufacturer's exposure to class-action lawsuits.

My legal advisors, a couple guys who say they can beat any ticket for $59 and a twelve-pack, wish me to add this important disclaimer:

This has been a comical safety announcement. If you mistook this for serious journalism, please stop reading and contact your local mental health authorities for further instructions.

SPACE JUNK

N EWS FROM NASA AND THE National Research Council has erased all my worries that I might one day be hit by a bus. I'm also no longer concerned about random acts of terror, outliving Social Security benefits, contracting West Nile virus, ingesting arsenic from my lipstick, choking in my sleep (with or without assistance), and that crazy-talking supermarket checker dude with the walleye. Those threats are nothing next to the thought of intercepting falling space debris with my noggin.

When NASA issued a warning that remnants of the Upper Atmosphere Research Satellite, and by remnants I mean particles as large as a mini-bus and weighing up to 300 pounds, were expected to soon collide with Earth, I thought I'd misread the alert. The space agency went so far as to list the odds of any individual being hit: one in 14 trillion. That number was later revised to a modest one in 3,200 by a different authority—possibly the same folks who're responsible for supplying U.S. unemployment numbers.

Considering a global population of 7 billion and that 75 percent of the planet is covered in water, NASA concluded there was no need for alarm. Safety in numbers, laws of permutations and combinations, and all that. The chances of being struck by space junk are no greater than winning the lottery (if you play it once instead of three times a week like those who expect the heavens to shower them with money instead of leftover satellite parts).

Depending on which set of odds you believe (1 in 14 trillion, or 1 in 3,200), the likelihood of being clobbered by falling rocket refuse could be as great as that of being killed by a natural disaster such as a hurricane, tornado, earthquake, or a Lady Gaga dress.

NASA has admitted there are currently over 22,000 catalogued space objects larger than four inches—they failed to state if that was diameter, circumference, or telescope width—being tracked by the U.S. Space Surveillance Network. This space junk is traveling at a rate of four to five miles per second, or roughly the speed of fuel price increases.

If my high school algebra skills are still accurate, a falling object the size of a bus, traveling at a rate of 14,400 mph (60 seconds multiplied by 4 multiplied by 60 minutes), dropped from five miles above Earth will make a hole the size of either a football field or Kansas. Either way, that's enough to produce a meteoric rise in home insurance premiums and cause a run on safety helmets.

But for me, the most unsettling part of all this was discovering there's a dedicated group of scientists responsible for tracking interstellar hazards. I mean, researchers have yet to agree on the impact of global warming, ozone depletion, or flash mobs. How can we rely on them to tell us when to duck?

I'm sure NASA knows how disturbing these disclosed dangers are for normal, law-abiding citizens who seldom notice anything above TV height. Evidence of that can be found on their website, where I found this question amid the FAQs:

Q: "Is re-entering debris a risk to people and property on Earth?"

The agency responded by assuring readers that one piece of catalogued space debris has fallen to Earth every day for the past 50 years. I don't know about you, but I take great comfort in knowing how many times I've already been missed. Nonetheless, isn't that kind of like telling me to take heart because none of the people (God help them) who've attempted to steal my identity have been successful? Of course, it's doubtful there have been that many attempts on my credit. Unlike space crap that'll land most anywhere, identity thieves have standards.

The space experts go on to say that no "serious injury" or "significant property damage" from space debris re-entry has been *confirmed.* Call me a stickler for words, but I would like to know their definitions for "serious," "significant," and "confirmed" before I give up practicing my ability to run in a serpentine fashion.

Satellite components that survive re-entry to the Earth's atmosphere are most likely, according to NASA, to strike sparsely populated areas like, and I'm quoting here, the Canadian Tundra, the Australian Outback, or Siberia. In other words, areas considered unimportant because a quarter of all Americans cannot locate them on a map.

You might think that after being fined $400 for "littering" the western Australian city of Esperance with the 1979 remains of Skylab, the U.S. would sense the gravity of this situation. Sadly, our government merely acknowledged that Australians have a sense of humor.

NASA's past neglect has prompted The National Research Council to order them to improve their "post-mission disposal standards." Don't laugh. Someone used your tax dollars to coin that term.

So, come on, space jockeys! Stop firing off what you refuse to clean up. And that goes for all you private enterprises too. I don't care if some commercial operation sent James Doohan's (the actor who played Scotty on *Star Trek*) ashes into space. It took a rocket to finally beam him there, and no doubt some of it, unlike the Starship Enterprise, *will* return to Earth.

I don't doubt that many a man would love to give his wife or girlfriend a galactic send-off of such proportions, and vice versa. However, there are better and cheaper ways to accomplish that. Not that I'd ever entertain them. Just sayin'...

On its website, NASA states that "Since 1988 the official policy of the United States has been to minimize the creation of new orbital debris." Existing debris is presumably being ignored because the only solution they have for its disposal is, "Eh, let's see where it lands. Maybe it'll strike the Taliban."

But that's not enough. We need everyone, including private companies, to control their space pollution. Just because some guy threatens to send his wife to the moon doesn't mean such trips should be made possible. Already the government has created too much revolving waste. We don't need private sector rocket scientists adding to it.

What's going to happen when there's so much space garbage out there that the aliens can't safely visit us anymore? No, not the ones from beyond our national borders. I'm talking about the little green men from Mars and Greys from Roswell.

If UFOs can no longer enter the Earth's atmosphere, our survival will be dependent on only human intelligence. And if you're reading this, I don't think I need to explain the direness of that proposition. All I know is that if something unexpected is going to punch through the clouds, I'd prefer it be hope for humanity instead of grave reminders of Isaac Newton.

I'd write more about interstellar risks, but right now I need to research which firm manufactures the best crash helmets.

THE DRAWER OF DOOM

E VERYBODY HAS ONE, I PRESUME. You know...that drawer where you toss appliance warranties, user manuals, and miscellaneous instruction booklets? Please tell me you know what I'm talking about and that I'm not the only one who saves these documents. Periodically, it's a good idea to sort through and dispose of any outdated materials. In other words, if you find a warranty for that VCR you bought in 1998, it's probably safe to let that go. However, I sometimes find myself in actual need of one of these rarely referenced materials. This morning was one such occasion.

Having spilled from my bedroom and into the kitchen, I noted the house felt extremely cold. I thought that perhaps my husband had forgotten to pull the door tight when he left for work. No, the latch appeared secure.

A check of the nearby thermostat revealed the heater wasn't working...on a morning when temperatures were below freezing outdoors. My kitchen was now a frigid 60 degrees.

Being cold natured, I immediately lit the gas fireplace to lessen any chance of frostbite. Next, I attempted to reignite the furnace, to no avail. The furnace, from what I could tell, had gone kaput overnight—kind of like my eyesight.

I needed my morning caffeine before tackling The Dreaded Drawer of Doom. Evidence of any repair history would be found inside that long-neglected space. I grabbed a soda, plopped two slices of bread into the toaster oven, and set a few strips of bacon in the nuke box before emptying the warranty drawer of its contents.

A beep sounded. Checking the bacon, I returned the strips to the microwave for another five seconds.

With any luck, I hoped to find a ten-year furnace warranty amid my pile of papers. For *this* house, I mean. Given my filing history, it wouldn't have surprised me to have unearthed one from a previous residence.

The more pamphlets I sifted through, the more I wondered if I might next be featured on a TV show about hoarders. At the time I saved some of these materials, I had to have been blind, stupid, or drunk. Why would I have needed to retain the assembly instructions for a lighted Christmas decoration that included only two pieces: a deer-shaped head and body? Worse yet, I'd kept the folded guide from the remote control that operated our outdoor Christmas lights. That printed paper included such necessary directions as "Push the ON button to turn on power." The Mr. Coffee manual cautioned me not to "touch the coffeemaker's hot surfaces." How ridiculous. I wouldn't know which surfaces were hot if I didn't first touch them.

Accompanying these documents were several "product registration" cards, which could easily substitute for a U.S. Census questionnaire. Why does Whirlpool need to know the ages of my children, my household income, or my I.Q.? No, they didn't come right out and ask for the I.Q., but if I completed and returned that card to the manufacturer, my intelligence level would be obvious.

No joke, I found a brochure titled "Know Your Can Opener." After all these years of familiar touching, I hadn't even bothered to learn the proper names for this appliance's parts. Sadder still, I'd never known there was a way to lengthen its cord.

The turkey fryer owner's manual could have been summed up in six words: *Do not use under any circumstances.* My toaster oven's "Use and Care Guide" provided such good advice as, "Do not operate in the presence of explosives." A slow cooker manual included pictorial instructions to help me identify the product's base, handles, lid, and control panel, which included all of three separate buttons. Under the "Precautions" section, I found the following helpful tip: "If using a specific recipe, one item may be substituted for another if equal quantity is used."

Who writes these things? The folks who craft IRS tax form instructions?

My thoughts were accompanied by a low humming noise. I'd been only vaguely aware of this sound for the last several minutes. Not until I smelled smoke did I make a connection.

The microwave had been running the entire time I spent sifting through the drawer!

I hit the "off" button, which I found without referring to any instruction manual. I'd inadvertently set the microwave to run for five *minutes* instead of five seconds. My bacon, the paper towels, and the parched plate that sported the remains of my breakfast were charred black. Embers glowed as I reached for the oven door. The rush of air when I opened the unit transformed those orange dots into full-fledged flames.

Within a few seconds, the fire died. I grabbed a potholder and hastened the remains to the kitchen sink. Dowsing the now unidentifiable substance with water, I extinguished any further safety threats. From the microwave oven, that is. *I* remained a potential hazard.

Never did I uncover the furnace warranty. Another few minutes of searching and I wouldn't have needed it anyhow.

HALCION DAZE

MY DENTIST ASSURED ME THAT he would administer Halcion before oral surgery. I'd had the drug once before, but I recalled nothing about it—which, I guess, is kind of the objective.

A molar had recently decided to part ways with me, even after I'd treated it like a princess. Years earlier, at great expense, the tooth had been crowned. Now, thanks to this ingrate, I needed a jawbone graft and a dental implant. And unfortunately, I wasn't a candidate for anesthesia because I have a problem with needles.

Needles can be lethal, even to those who aren't on death row. That's how I look at them. Each one has the potential to *kill* me. So nobody wants to stick me with a needle unless he or she first sedates me with a strong narcotic or ball-peen hammer. The carpenter's tool would probably work best because it takes a lot to knock me down. However, I much prefer the medication route.

All kinds of fears about Halcion surfaced after my initial consultation with my dentist. What if I talked during my drug-induced state? Might I mention something embarrassing, like that recent bikini-wax incident that had left me as naked as a groomed poodle? What if I got so relaxed while inhaling gas that I expelled a little of my own? Even more disquieting, what would happen if my husband decided to take advantage of my condition? If he spent a full day aimlessly relaxing instead of working through my "honey-do" list, might that set a precedent of some sort?

But most importantly, I wondered what would happen if the Halcion didn't work.

When I next saw my daughter-in-law, Julie, I expressed a few of these concerns. (Not the bikini one, of course.) She and my son Ron had both undergone dental procedures during the past few months, but I couldn't recall if either of them had been given oral sedation.

Julie laughed sheepishly when I told her I would be receiving Halcion. I immediately registered this as a bad sign. Then she told me what had happened to Ron when he'd been under the influence of this drug, one the FDA has said can impair "psychomotor performance."

Let me preference this story with some relevant background. Ron is a police officer who participates in extreme sports, runs marathons, and functions at only two speeds: hyper-alert and Is-that-a-corpse. Unlike mine, his body systems are so pure that even baby aspirin runs the risk of being a hallucinogenic. Nonetheless, some dental procedures—I would suggest *all*—simply shouldn't be undertaken without pharmaceuticals. Thus, Ron was given a Halcion pill prior to oral mutilation...I mean, dental surgery.

Julie had been the designated driver, making her, possibly for the first time ever, responsible for Ron's behavior. She'd been advised not to let Ron out of her sight while he was under the effects of Halcion. Given his inert condition after the procedure, Julie assumed the dentist liked to err on the side of caution. Ron seemed groggy yet awake enough to ask for a chocolate shake. He was a tough guy, probably strong enough to override whatever others experienced from the drug.

Being a good wife, Julie drove Ron and their nine-year-old son, Heath, to a nearby ice cream parlor. Entering the strip mall, she noted a furniture store. After purchasing treats for Ron and Heath, she checked to see where she might park Ron while she explored furnishings. Seldom did they venture into that part of Dallas, so Julie didn't want to miss checking out the store.

An astute furniture store owner had stationed a park bench right outside the storefront. Julie led Ron and Heath to the bench, where she gave Heath instructions to watch his father.

"*Don't* let him get up or go anywhere," she commanded. "Daddy isn't supposed to be alone right now. Okay?"

Heath nodded and continued eating his ice cream.

"Will you be okay?" Julie asked Ron.

"Uh-huh," Ron muttered, sipping his shake through a straw.

"I'll be right back," Julie said.

As she told me the story, Julie's eyes revealed her shame. "I was only gone for maybe fifteen minutes. It really wasn't very long at all."

Returning to the bench where she'd left Ron and Heath, Julie found only a shell of her husband. His head tilted sideways, feet splayed haphazardly on the sidewalk in front of him, eyes at half-mast, he sat barely clutching his cardboard cup. A river of chocolate ice cream snaked from his lips to his chin.

"He looked like a stroke victim," Julie said. "I could just imagine what people who passed him must have thought. 'Somebody left that poor handicapped man sitting there trying to feed himself.'"

Needless to say, Julie was perplexed by her son's failure to notice his dad's mental departure. "Heath, how could you let your dad sit here like this?"

Heath blinked and then matter-of-factly replied, "You told me not to let him go anywhere. He didn't get up."

Hearing this tale, I realized I needed to be sure my husband didn't abandon me in a public place while I was loopy on sedatives.

On the day of surgery, I greeted the oral surgeon with trepidation. "I'm difficult to put under," I warned him. "I get so wired that the drugs sometimes don't take effect."

"Oh, that's all right," he said. "I'm used to that. My wife's the same way."

"Yes, but have you ever done surgery on her?"

"Uh-huh, I have...right here in this office. And she kept telling me that she was still feeling pain, though I imagine it was only pressure, and so she kept asking me for another shot, and because I wanted to keep her calm, I gave it to her." He shook his head. "When I was finished, she said she had to go the restroom. My assistant led her there and asked if she needed help, but she said she didn't." The surgeon chuckled. "Someone heard a thud, and then she wouldn't answer when I knocked and called her name. I had to break down the door." He stared off down the hallway. "There she was, face down, pants around her ankles, right where she'd passed out."

Now, maybe I'm peculiar, but this wasn't exactly the kind of story that inspired confidence. "May I go to the restroom now?" I wanted to be sure to get that out of the way before I had to swallow some pride along with my medicine.

When I returned from doing my duty, a dental assistant ground two blue pills into a powder and told me to open my mouth and lift my tongue.

"Are you giving me *two* Halcion pills?" I asked.

"Yes."

"Why did you crush them?" I asked. "By the way, I only swallowed *one* pill last time. I've never had two at once."

"This is what the doctor wants you to have. We crush them and put the powder under your tongue to help it absorb into your bloodstream fast."

I hesitantly accepted the Halcion, along with two antibiotics and some Ibuprofen.

"Tell my husband not to set me anyplace in public when I leave," I pleaded.

The assistant looked askance at me. "The doctor is visiting with him now," she said. "He's going over all your aftercare instructions."

After that, events get fuzzy. I remember being pushed in a wheelchair to the car. I seem to recall feeling something cold on my face. Hubby later explained that he drove through a fast food restaurant and bought me a shake. He denies leaving me alone with it for any amount of time. He also claims he didn't consume any of that indulgent treat. One of those statements holds some likelihood of truth.

Five hours after I returned home, I woke up. And five days later, I felt like being conscious. Trust me on this one. Nobody should undergo this procedure unless he or she is faced with a choice between a jawbone graft and a feeding tube. That operation wasn't one for Pretty Girls.

My face swelled to double its normal size. I looked like the Godmother, and I don't mean the fairytale type. Dogs would have cowered and children cried for their mamas if I could have summoned the strength to leave my bed.

I couldn't see inside my mouth because my jaw wouldn't open wide enough to even slip in a spoon, much less a mirror. But when I finally could hold a flashlight to my lips, I dared to survey the damage. As best I could tell, a molar and one wisdom tooth had been replaced by a beef tenderloin. The stitches appeared to have been strung through my gums by a member of the Meatpackers Union.

One week later, when I finally felt like venturing past the sofa, I searched for my car keys but couldn't find them. Thinking back, I recalled that on the day of my dental surgery, Hubby had driven home in my car. He had to have misplaced my key ring. Given his memory, I held little hope of ever again engaging my car's ignition.

I called him at work. "Do you have any idea where my car keys are? You must have driven home with them last week when you took me for surgery."

"Sure. They're in my left bathroom drawer."

"Why would you put my car keys in your bathroom

drawer?" I couldn't wait to hear his explanation.

"Because the dentist told me to hide the keys from you."

If there's ever a next time, I'm going to request aftercare instructions that include abundant rest and the avoidance of all housework.

DANGEROUS ATTRACTIONS

I SET THE GLASS OF SALTWATER next to the sink and hesitated. Having recently undergone oral surgery and a jawbone graft, I'd been instructed to rinse my mouth with this nasty-tasting concoction several times a day. Since I couldn't justify a trip to the tropics, where I normally succumb to sipping seawater, I had stirred a teaspoon of table salt into some filtered H_2O and improvised.

I would soon need the mixture again, so I left the remains on the counter.

Then, I thought, what if someone found the glass and took a swig before I could warn him or her of the invisible contents? Other than the potential entertainment value, I feared such an incident could produce unintended results—and possibly extra bathroom detail. I remembered the time my youngest child swallowed too much of the Gulf of Mexico. That outcome has been described in my previous book, *Crap Chronicles*. Suffice it to say, his clothes had to be discarded and the car fumigated.

At the moment, though, I was the only one home. The risks, I decided, were nil. I certainly would not mistake that salty blend for spring water. Vodka, perhaps, but never Ozarka. But I couldn't afford to mix alcohol with my pain medications. So I'd be safe, if insufficiently numb.

My concern over unattended, partially filled drinking glasses has a backstory. As a toddler, I'd almost been done in by a cupful of mystery liquid.

A handyman of sorts, my father seldom put away his tools or cleaned up after himself. When I was two years old, he embarked on a project that involved the use of paint thinner. I'm sure I inhaled the fumes, which could explain my attraction to Sharpie pens. Dad used one of my plastic drinking mugs to portion out the paint thinner. He later set the cup on our kitchen countertop. Within my reach. This negligence resulted in my first emergency room visit and Dad's last unrestricted access to the cupboards.

Comparing then and now, I reassured myself that no one would need to have his stomach pumped for drinking my saltwater. That was not to say that stomach contents might not need to be *emptied*. But if so, at least it would be in a more *natural* way.

I recalled another case of mistaken fluids, this one involving a Pepsi bottle and my mother, who had a bad habit of drinking whatever others failed to finish.

In my early twenties, I had been visiting my parents' house on a hot summer day when my brother Kerry decided to work on his motorcycle. From my vantage point in the living room, I saw him enter the kitchen. He studied the room and snatched an empty soda bottle from the countertop. As the oldest and self-declared superior of four children, I took little interest in his actions. For all I knew, he could have been looking for a target (other than me) at which to shoot.

Minutes later, Kerry trailed back through the

kitchen. I heard him set down something, possibly that bottle, and leave. Distracted by what my infant son had unloaded in his diaper, I didn't see what Kerry had deposited on the countertop.

Mom passed through the living room and into the kitchen, stopping briefly to interact with her grandson. She rounded the corner and then momentarily vanished from sight. I heard the refrigerator door open and close. Possibly Mom had taken a drink of some refreshing beverage.

She returned to the back bedrooms, where she'd been futilely cleaning. With my dad and three brothers as cohabitants, to gain any household order would have required combustible fuels. However, my brothers had already used up all the available gasoline and found other uses for the matches.

Kerry came back in, scanned the kitchen, scratched his head, and sauntered back outside. I continued crocheting an afghan to cover the hole in my hand-me-down sofa.

About an hour later, I heard Mom open the fridge door. She choked and gagged, sounding as if she might have swallowed antifreeze. But what she'd imbibed had been something equally, if not more, unappealing.

Standing over the sink, Mom hacked and spit. "AUGH!" she cried between dry heaves.

Kerry strode through the back door. "What's wrong?" Then he saw the Pepsi bottle he'd been searching for earlier. His eyes flashed a giant GUILTY sign.

"I'm going to kill you!" Mom shouted, which was a common threat that no one in our family ever took seriously. "What *is* this?" She pointed to the Pepsi bottle she'd ditched in the sink.

"Why would you drink a hot Pepsi, anyway?" Kerry asked.

Mom coughed several times and then wiped her tongue with a dish towel. "It was in the refrigerator!"

"Well, who put it in there?"

Mom threw her arms wide. "I did!"

"I left it on the countertop for a *reason*!"

Mom studied Kerry as if he were a felon.

"I was going to pour the oil out of it later," he explained. Kerry's frown gave way to a grin that erupted into a full donkey bray. "See what happens when you put half-empty bottles back into the fridge?"

As it turned out, Kerry had drained his used motorcycle oil into the Pepsi bottle. Mom had spotted the bottle and, thinking it contained her favorite beverage, put the drink in the refrigerator.

No serious injury occurred. Though Mom had trust issues for quite a while thereafter, on the upside, she clocked many more miles over four subsequent decades—and she never needed an oil change.

I forgot all about my saltwater and never got around to reusing it or to rinsing the glass. My mouth hurt too much to worry about such matters. I still had stitches in my gums and didn't want to risk bursting any of them while reminiscing about Mom coating her throat with motor lubricant.

That night, I climbed into bed, hoping my pain medication would kick in soon. Hubby ambled through the bedroom and into the adjacent bathroom. I heard him brush his teeth and open his pill container.

"ACK! SPLUH! HAWWWW! What the *hell* is in this stuff?"

I clutched my jaws to stifle a laugh.

"Why would you leave a glass of *salt*water on the counter?" he demanded, still retching.

"Why would you pick up something that's sitting on the sink and *drink* it?" I fired back.

"Because it looked like plain *water*."

"Yeah, well, count yourself lucky that it wasn't paint thinner."

The moral to this story is this: Don't ask whether a glass is half empty or half full. It's more important to find out who last set it down and if the contents are safe to drink.

BOOZING BARBADOS

WHEN MY HUSBAND AND I booked a trip to Barbados, we never anticipated danger. Memories of previous travel disasters had long since faded. What could possibly go wrong? It was May, the "dry season," and we were vacationing outside the hurricane belt.

The weather offered the first hint of our miscalculation. The day we arrived, rain fell so hard that streets flooded. Our hotel receptionist said she couldn't answer questions about tomorrow's weather, but she suggested we enjoy the resort's generous lounge and cheap drinks.

At the hotel bar, we met a Canadian couple.

"It's odd to see storms this time of year," my husband said.

The man and his wife exchanged a bewildered look. "We've been here *nine* days," the woman said. "It's been like this every day."

As the showers continued, we huddled under the bar area's thatched roof and listened to a local singer. The entertainer moved seamlessly between reggae music and John Denver's *Take Me Home*—which pretty much mirrored my thinking right then. The crowd applauded and hooted when the performer sang that long forgotten tune. But

I hadn't flown 2,700 miles to hear John Denver music. Briefly, I considered banging my head on the table until he stopped slaughtering that melody. If there's anything that sounds more incongruent than a native islander crooning country songs, I've haven't yet encountered it.

For the next two days, the heavens offered an abundance of "liquid sunshine." On day three, we waved goodbye to the Canadians as they merrily caught a taxi to the airport. "Good luck," they called to us from their cab.

"It looks like this has set in for the duration," I said to my husband as I scanned the dark skies. "Maybe we should take a tour or something. There's not going to be much sunbathing."

Expecting to get wet, one way or the other, we booked a snorkel cruise that advertised a half-day excursion, two snorkel stops, and free snacks and booze. This would allow us to see something beyond the resort and any *American Idol* hopefuls they might have hired as entertainers.

Immediately after we boarded the private craft, we met two people who appeared to have forgotten to disembark from the previous tour. The man, who we soon learned was named Ray, and his partner, who I shall refer to as Ray's Gal, were already ripe for sailing as they were both three sheets to the wind.

I'd guess Ray's age to be about 65, and his partner might have been a couple years younger. Both spoke with British accents as they jointly explained that one could sing and the other could dance. Ray's Gal demonstrated by humping Ray from behind in "dirty dog" fashion. From the looks of it, she probably would have been more at home grinding against the ship's mast.

I observed a Bob Marley tattoo inked on Ray's bare chest. A long blond rat tail hung from his nape, in contrast to the top of his head where he'd begun to bald. Presumably, he was growing what was left of his mane to compensate for the part that had already galloped away.

Ray's Gal looked like a rock star groupie from the 1960s. Her bleached platinum locks stopped at her shoulders, but her juvenile behavior revealed no discernible limits.

Right off, Ray asked my profession. I presume he'd ruled out "party girl" from the modest swimsuit and cover-up I was wearing. "I'm an author," I said, which instantly prompted him to ask me to write his story—provided he could remember it.

"Ah've hawd an interestin' loff," Ray boasted.

No doubt, he was telling the truth. Unfortunately, he fell asleep before he could share much about his past.

One of the crewmen offered plastic cups filled with juice. My companion and I partook of this refreshing beverage, a combination of pineapple juice and coconut rum. The mixture seemed rather tame and left no alcohol aftertaste.

I had a second one.

Hubby had a third.

Now, as anyone who's ever drunk coconut rum and pineapple juice can attest, the effects of that beverage are much the same as those of a Demerol injection. This potent drink catches up to you and strikes you stupid before you've had time to reveal that on your own. The act of standing (or swimming) seems to accentuate the results, meaning that you really shouldn't try to snorkel after consuming this relaxant...unless, of course, you have a life vest or a death wish. My man had neither when he ventured overboard during the second snorkel stop.

I didn't see Hubby depart, but at some point I noted he was no longer aboard the boat. A group of Europeans had been conversing with me while sharing enough second-hand smoke to signal nautical distress. I excused myself to enter the waves and look for my missing spouse, who I guessed might be floating out to sea unnoticed.

The cool ocean temperature shocked me partially sober as I battled the modest swells. Some forty yards from the beach, I fought to glimpse the shoreline. No sign of blue swim trunks anywhere. Apparently, Mr. Adventure hadn't gone ashore.

I struggled against the waves, propelling my way toward the shore. Without my snorkel fins, I barely made any headway. I should return to the boat before I drowned, I decided.

Almost there! I kicked toward the ship with what little reserves I had, keeping my eyes trained on the ocean floor for Hubby's blue swimsuit. Drawing close, I noticed the bottom of the craft in front of me was black.

Our cruise vessel had a green hull! This wasn't the right boat!

I had swum thirty yards the wrong way and had to retrace my path. If I didn't sink before this ordeal was over, it would be because of my built-in pontoons. Silently, I gave thanks to my maker for giving me a butt fat enough to float.

Ten minutes later, seated on the deck, I rehearsed the story I'd tell the children when I arrived home. "Your father went out to view a few fish and never came back. We had to give up the search when the boat ran out of booze."

I was still mentally cursing Hubby's carefree spirit when I heard someone say, "Oo-oo, that's a nasty cut."

Looking up from my despair, I observed my MIA spouse climbing aboard the craft, his forehead scraped, shins scuffed and bleeding.

"I fell down inside the fort," he said, laughing as though that were some kind of punch line.

I glared at him, unsure whether to be angry or enthused by his sudden reappearance. On the one hand, I'd been reunited with my spouse. On the other, he'd irritated me with his casual dismissal of what appeared to be an attention-worthy injury. "What fort?" I asked.

"The one on shore," he said, pointing at a half-excavated pile of ruins.

"Why would you go in *there*?"

He bent and dabbed at his leg with a napkin someone supplied. "Why do people climb Mount Kilimanjaro?"

"I don't know," I said, "but they don't do it *drunk*!"

"Yeah," Hubby said. "I kept falling on the rocks and sliding back down the hill and having to start all over again."

I had to wonder, given the way he looked, if he'd bothered to remove his fins before climbing. At that moment, I didn't care what he did for the rest of the snorkel excursion. Instead, I focused on my cup of pineapple juice and coconut rum—which was a challenging enough task. The drink seemed to magically refill itself whenever I wasn't looking. Another round of that tonic and I'd be as fast asleep as Ray.

A loud horn sounded nearby.

"What was that?" I asked a deck hand.

"A conch shell," he said.

"No way!"

"Hey, give me that shell," the ship's mate called to his captain. He retrieved the conch and blew into it, duplicating the sound I'd heard earlier. "Here, you do it," he said, handing me the shell. "All you have to do is blow in this end and make a fart sound with your mouth."

I did as he'd instructed, pretending the shell was a trumpet.

Baroooooom!

"I did it!" I said, unsure who was the more shocked.

The ship's mate put one hand on Hubby's shoulder, bent to look him in the eyes, and said, "You're a lucky man, my friend."

Ray briefly regained consciousness, looked at me through half-closed lids, and slurred, "Ah won ta mahry you!"

The deck hand whispered to me, "We always make the men's drinks stronger so we can get them drunk and steal their women."

Should you ever go to Barbados, consider yourself forewarned.

NO DAY AT THE CIRCUS

EVERY TIME I DRIVE PAST a historical marker, I get a little twitchy. Forced during much of my childhood to read roadside signs while standing barefoot on the shoulder of some obscure highway, I no longer care who won a Comanche battle or what the Corps of Engineers did in the 1800s to wreck the national landscape. I don't want anyone to make me read about it, either. If I desired to know that sort of information, I'd have majored in history instead of disco.

My father, The Walking Encyclopedia, is quite the opposite. He has spent his entire life consuming facts and figures with which, I presume, to impress others. I'm not sure who those others are because I've never overheard anyone say, "Oh, that's amazing!" when he cites the height of the tallest hill in Texas, some city's precise elevation level, or the life expectancy of a spotted salamander. But I imagine somewhere out there in Nerdville there's at least one interested party. Dad has spent a lifetime preparing to meet that person.

Having a father like mine assured that I'd never see Disneyland before I could legally drive. That establishment offered no museums or historical markers. Perhaps if Mickey had performed a Civil

War reenactment, Dad would have been more open to my suggestion to visit the land of Prince Charming. Instead, our family of six vacationed every year for two weeks, and I seldom saw anything remotely entertaining—other than Mom and Dad yelling at each other over a map.

Dad did all the driving. Mom didn't learn to steer anything larger than a baby stroller until she was in her thirties. But that wasn't uncommon for the times. Mom's job was to simply keep up with the four kids and provide a scapegoat for Dad to yell at when he got lost, which happened frequently.

Somehow, before the invention of GPS, we managed to tour from Texas to the Seattle World's Fair (where I was denied any thrill rides), San Antonio's HemisFair '68 (where I viewed only the international exhibits), and multiple iterations of Nashville's Grand Ole Opry (wherein I slept through Minnie Pearl's, Grandpa Jones's, and no telling who else's performances).

We explored the battlegrounds of Gettysburg, and Dad took photos of us children perched on artifacts. "Get over there and climb on that cannon," he would say. I'm not sure in what way he thought any of us would benefit from learning to mount artillery. Possibly he was readying his kids for a career in the military. Or maybe the porn industry. Either way, none of us took that hint.

Driving between points of interest, Dad would yell, "Kids, wake up! There's a historical marker coming up!"

I don't know whose idea it was to announce a road sign with another road sign, but I would beat him with a buggy whip if I could discover his identity. I'd first have to locate a buggy whip, but I'm sure Dad could tell me where to find one.

Four children, two adults, three suitcases, six blankets and pillows, a cooler, lantern, camp stove, and a canvas tent the size of Rhode Island made for a full automobile. The tent and camping equipment were strapped to the overhead luggage rack, which always made for a fun setup after we'd driven through a thunderstorm. In the station wagon's rear storage area, the suitcases formed a support under all the pillows and blankets. While Dad drove, I and at least one of my three younger brothers slept on top of that mound of bedding, our bodies slow-roasting under the glass-filtered sunshine, ignoring most of the scenery Dad had spent his annual savings to show us.

While our entire family stood roadside looking as though our car might have broken down, Dad would direct, "Diana, read the sign out loud for your brothers." Usually I had been asleep, which left me barely able to see for the sunlight glinting off the metal monument. My feet burned against the scorching road cinders. All I wanted to do was climb back inside the station wagon before one of my brothers stole my place atop the suitcases. We operated on squatter's rights. Whenever I was late returning to the car, I'd have to wait for the next monument or museum to appear before I could reclaim my position.

To Dad, educational opportunities abounded in the most boring settings. Thus, I was introduced to more governors' mansions and dead Presidents' homes than I could muster the strength to sulk through.

Once, we went to Washington, D.C., to see where the current President resided—which garnered my interest. Sadly, we never quite made it to the White House because we couldn't find our way out of the city's roundabouts. The counterclockwise traffic flow confused my father so badly, and he drove in circles for so long, that the whole family begged for mercy. "Forget the White House," we pleaded. "We're too dizzy to appreciate it, anyhow."

After spending so many vacation days observing overrated historic tourist sites, I was elated when Dad announced we were going to see Ringling Bros. and Barnum & Bailey Circus. At last, he'd chosen an attraction for which I could gather some excitement. My chest swelled with pride, just thinking Daddy was taking us—forget *us*, he was taking *me*—to the circus!

However, it was a l-o-n-g way to that Big Top.

Dad drove and drove and drove, and then we camped, packed up the tent the next morning, and were propelled still farther down the road. We motored all the way from Dallas, Texas, to Sarasota, Florida, home of Ringling Brothers headquarters.

I'm sure we stopped a few times to read historical markers, but I didn't even mind. I was on my way to see the circus!

When Dad pulled the car into the Ringling Brothers parking lot, I saw no sign of a circus tent. No elephants graced the periphery. Nobody passed by on stilts. I didn't even detect a whiff of cotton candy.

"I don't see any circus here," I complained.

"You don't?" Dad asked. "Well, it's sitting right here. See the sign?" He pointed to a billboard-sized depiction of The Greatest Show on Earth. "We have to go inside."

But the facility contained only more pictures of circuses and various Ringling Brothers memorabilia. My sole memory of the place has been reduced to a Plexiglas-ensconced shoe that had once belonged to the tallest man in the world. Adjacent to that gargantuan lace-up boot stood a black and white photo of the guy who'd once worn that accessory. However, nowhere was the man himself to be seen. In fact, the display information stated he no longer lived. "Where's the circus?" I kept asking.

"It's touring the U.S.," a female docent replied. "The circus is here during wintertime, and it travels the country during the summer."

Despondent, I realized that Dad had driven us to the Ringling Brothers Circus *Museum* instead of The Greatest Show on Earth. The circus was probably making its way toward Dallas, even as I stood there wanting to throw a temper tantrum of epic proportions. I didn't dare act on that desire, though, for fear my father might leave me behind to be raised by The Missing Link.

After that major disappointment, the family continued traveling south to Key West, where apparently there wasn't much to see. My only recollection is of the car tires drumming over an endless row of bridges. Perhaps I was so depressed that I slept through that part of the vacation.

Other children my age arrived home from their travels with fascinating tales from places like

Mammoth Cave or Disneyland or Coney Island. I had nothing to offer. None of my friends wanted to hear about the house where Lincoln last dined with his stepmother. My classmates boasted of fun times, cool souvenirs, and giant swirly lollipops. The only vacation mementos I had were a strand of bruises I'd suffered while sleeping on the ground.

Now, I realize many children never experience family vacations, and I don't want to sound like an ingrate. During my childhood, I learned many facts and witnessed a great deal of American history. Unfortunately, I can't recall any of it now. Remembering my vacations with Mom and Dad, I hoped to create similar experiences with my own brood. Not the kind where we all slept in a tent and argued over which way was North, but rather the ones where we dozed to prevent being clobbered for chanting "Are we there yet?"

My first vacation with my husband and children took us to Disney World. Like Dad, we drove all the way from Texas to Florida. Only, instead of a station wagon, we traveled in a minivan and stayed overnight in hotels.

On the way to Florida, one of the children shouted from the back seat, "Stop! There's a state marker ahead! Let's go stand in front of it!"

Hubby pulled to the shoulder, while I sat dumbfounded. He and two children climbed from the van and ran to the Louisiana border sign, where they spun and waited for me to snap their photos.

Someday one of them will likely write about how lame that was.

PHOTO ABOVE: This was as close as I ever came to seeing
Ringling Bros. and Barnum & Bailey Circus.

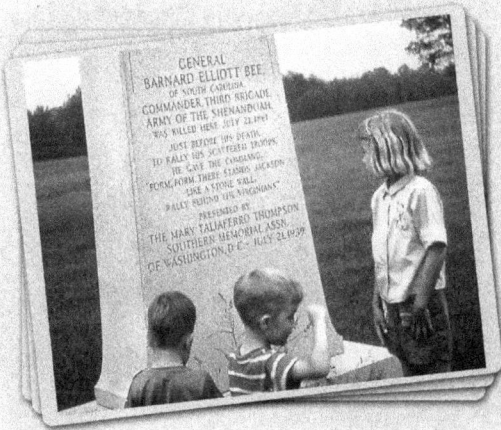

PHOTO ABOVE: Most of my vacation time was spent
reading historical signs and monuments.

PHOTO ABOVE: My brother Kerry didn't like the cannons either.

DYES AND DECEPTION

I F HE DIDN'T WANT HIS head to look as if it had been dunked in a punchbowl, then my husband should have asked someone else to dye his hair. I am not a hairdresser. I can't even get my own hair color right, which is why I pay somebody else to do it.

I used to think I could save money by using those hair-frosting kits sold to anyone who lacks fear of failure and a beautician's license. But after two attempts to add blond highlights to my locks, I concluded beauty school might have been a viable alternative to college after all. Instead of looking sun-kissed, I appeared carrot-clobbered.

The orange streaks I'd accidentally produced during my early twenties were next to impossible to conceal. For months thereafter, I'd darkened my tresses with temporary hair color and avoided being seen in daylight. I'd forgotten to share those stories with my current spouse.

Seated at the dinner table, my husband casually commented about his work day. "I met Robert [not his real name] today. He's nearly sixty, and he doesn't have a single gray hair on his head." He set down his fork and stared out the kitchen window. "I don't get it. How is it that none of the older guys at work have gray hair? I'm the only one who does."

After several rounds of layoffs during which many over age 50 had been let go, the answer was clear. Silver hair attracts the attention of those in charge of workforce reductions. That's why astute executives who want to keep their jobs make frequent investments in Clairol.

"Surely you realize they're all dyeing their hair," I said.

Hubby winced. "You think so?"

"Of course."

"Maybe I should think about coloring mine too, then. Does your hairdresser dye men's hair?"

I didn't know, but I agreed to check. When I next visited the salon, I asked my stylist about men's hair color.

"Oh, most men just use the box kind," she said. "But I have this one guy who brings the box to me and has me put it on for him." She chuckled. "He doesn't want his wife to know he's dyeing his hair."

I suspected that man didn't want his wife to know a great deal more than that. Who was dyeing the rest of his hair? Surely a spouse must be the first to notice when the carpet and drapes no longer matched.

On my way home from the salon, I stopped at a local drugstore and bought some packaged hair color in a shade I thought would work for my guy. His natural tint when we married had been almost black. To me, it had appeared jet black, but he'd insisted it was dark mocha. The color I chose was labeled "darkest brown." However, the hair color pictured on the box appeared black to my eyes, so it's possible that I don't see distinctions between dark colors.

We decided to dye Hubby's hair on a weekend to give me time to correct any mishaps that might occur. Also, we figured the break between coworker sightings would reduce the chance of anyone noticing.

And we were almost right.

"Leave it on a few minutes longer," he instructed when I suggested it was time to rinse off the color.

What could that hurt? Dark hair was dark hair, I figured. So I waited another five minutes before removing the lathery mix. But when I'd finished the job, I realized that instead of turning back the clock I'd made my spouse into a cult figure. He looked like Dracula.

To make matters worse, I'd also let the dye drip. Now the tops of his ears were four shades darker than his lobes. However, a great deal of scrubbing with a little fingernail polish remover took care of what could have been easily mistaken for liver spots.

"I sure hope nobody notices this and makes a big deal of it," he said, eyeing his reflection in the bathroom mirror.

"Don't worry. They'll ask if you got a haircut or something. But the truth is, nobody really looks at your hair when they see you. We think everyone inspects us thoroughly, but that's seldom true." I shook my head. "Most folks are too busy thinking about themselves to study you that hard."

The following Monday, The Count sneaked into the workplace and remained in his office for most of the day. Eventually, though, he had a face-to-face meeting.

A female peer remarked, "Weeellll, it looks like

we have a new employee!"

Only a woman would have said that. Proof of this occurred when one of Hubby's male staff saw him and asked, "Did you shave off your mustache?"

He hadn't worn a mustache in fifteen years.

Within a few weeks, Hubby's hair lightened to the point that it looked more natural. But by the time that happened, another dose of Clairol was needed. This time, he asked me to remove the color *early*.

Unfortunately, the shorter processing time failed to darken all the gray. His crown was a deep shade of chocolate, but his hairline remained silver. If he'd stuck a raccoon on top of his head, he would have looked more normal. Nonetheless, he decided to remain Jimmy Two-Tone for a while.

Included in his recent dye kit was a two-week "touch-up" color to be used between full applications. Thinking this might cover the remaining gray, Hubby decided to use the touch-up...and to do the job himself. The instructions said to rub in the color and rinse ten minutes later.

He stood before the bathroom mirror, his hands gloved in plastic, rubbing the product into his scalp. I noted the contents on his palms looked more like grape puree than hair dye, but I didn't worry. Whatever the outcome, it had to be an improvement.

After he'd dried his hair, my husband offered himself for inspection. "What do you think?"

I studied his head. "It's still a little gray around the edges. Turn around and let me see the back."

Now, I try never to say anything about the thin spot on the back of my man's head. He insists this patch doesn't exist in any place other than my imagination. But this time, I had to speak up.

"Omigod, you've dyed your scalp purple!"

"I'm not asking you about my scalp. How does my hair look?"

"Your hair looks fine. But your bald spot is *purple*."

He gave me an indignant look. "What bald spot?"

I lovingly spun him so his back was to the large mirror. I then presented him with my hand-held mirror. "Look at the back of your head."

A tennis-ball-sized space on his noggin shone bright burgundy. He looked as though he'd been accosted from behind by a plum-throwing assailant.

"It'll probably wash off in the shower," he said.

By the next day, I'd forgotten all about his newly acquired berry patch, and I slept right through my spouse's morning departure. So I was caught off-guard when he called me at 8:00 a.m., shrieking, "Why didn't you tell me my *hair* was purple too?"

Did I mention I have a difficult time distinguishing between dark-colored strands?

"It didn't look purple to me." If I'd pointed out his bald spot, why wouldn't I have told him if he looked like a punk rocker? His accusation seemed illogical.

"I just went to the bathroom and looked in the mirror, and the gray hairs are now *purple*." Hubby sighed. "What am I going to do now?"

"I don't know. Have you ever considered going blond?"

"I can't let anyone see me like this. I have to come home, say I'm sick or something. You've got to fix this *today*."

The most confusing part of all this was that my husband trusted me to make him look right—again. Hadn't I already botched all efforts to be his colorist?

I had to attribute his confidence to blind affection. I'm his wife, and he knows I love him enough to always keep his best interests at heart. He trusts me not to poison his food, ruin his laundry, or run off with the yard man. Consequently, he believes he can rely on me to not dye his hair purple. It's a logical leap, though a terribly flawed one.

Despite his misplaced faith, I knew someone else could do the task better than I could. "Why don't you call your stylist and have her do the correction?"

"No. I'm not doing that."

"Why not?"

"Are you kidding? She'd probably charge me a hundred dollars!"

Armed with a new box of color, I reluctantly prepped Hubby for yet another dye application. This time, I dipped a forefinger in petroleum jelly and traced his hairline and ears with it to form a protective barrier between his skin and the goo I was about to squirt on his head.

Approaching his crown, I stopped and stared at that vacant patch he refuses to acknowledge. The wine-colored hole in his hair begged my attention. Though the instructions specifically stated not to rub the dye into the scalp, I made an exception. If I massaged a small amount into that empty area, then his skin would darken to blend in with his hair. And then the bald circle would vanish from everyone else's sight. And if not, I planned to complete the job with a black marker.

When I'd finished with the dye, I washed my gullible spouse's hair and fanned his head with a blow dryer. We both inspected the color, which had turned out perfect. That balding place in the back of his head had all but disappeared, thanks to my blatant disregard of the instructions.

He raised a mirror to look at his crown. "The purple's all gone!"

"Only your hairdresser knows for sure," I said. But if I'd been honest, I'd have added, "And however many people read my next book."

A STEP SHY OF HUMAN

G O AHEAD AND SCAN MY retinas or take my thumbprints. Ask my first pet's name or my favorite teacher. But don't make me guess at scrambled computer security words. I cannot decipher them. For the record, I was never any good at finding Waldo, either.

Those blurry, crowded letters might just as well be ink blots or, given my work habits, lunch stains. They could even be the remains of a squashed housefly. This is what I want to tell website owners who use CAPTCHAs, those tricky, distorted letters and numbers intended to verify that users are humans, as opposed to, oh, I don't know, maybe zombies.

While searching online for theater tickets, I encountered the dreaded CAPTCHA barricade. Before I could access the purchase screen, I was asked to first solve a mystery word that had been obscured and compressed into a dark splotch.

"We need to know that you're not a 'bot,'" the website explained.

I'd been called a "snot" once (I'm sure it had been in jest), but never a "bot," so I expected to easily pass the hominid test. Squinting, I studied the muddled image. Nothing recognizable there. I closed one eye and leaned in closer to the monitor. Then I stuck out my tongue and pressed it against my upper lip. Don't ask me why. That trick had always worked for Mom.

Failing to distinguish an actual word, I donned my reading glasses. The lenses that normally brought my 27-inch monitor's display into sharper view were of no help this time. If there was a word hidden in that rectangular box, it had to have been written in Sanskrit or hieroglyphics or some language for which I had neither any comprehension nor the requisite computer keys to duplicate. Either that or I'd lost more vision than I was willing to admit.

Another ten or twelve attempts to deduce the skewed image brought me no closer to a solution. I pounded my fist against my desk. "Stop it!" I screamed at the imaginary troll inside my computer screen. "I want to buy these tickets now, before they sell out!"

Then, I noticed a button marked "Vision Impaired" and realized in a sad flash of unwelcomed awareness that I apparently met that description. I clicked the link. If this security feature could simply *speak* the words to me, then surely I could key the correct letters.

"Type the words you hear, separated by a space," the instructions advised.

I listened closely to the female voice. The last time I'd heard anything like that, I'd just asked a New York Transit Authority agent to give me directions. The woman had triggered her P.A. system, pressed the microphone to her nose, and slurred something unintelligible.

If I typed what I'd heard, it would have looked

like "fiereightrrg senialee zeronine," nonsensical syllables that made me wonder if my next visit should be to the Hearing Aid Center. To the right of the *Make-your-best-guess-Loser* box I saw another link labeled "New Words." Maybe the next round of auditory expressions would be more distinctive. I clicked the link and strained to hear the computer as it droned another phrase of gobbledygook.

"I'm never going to get these tickets if you don't stop *effing* with me." The automated voice might have been that of the GPS gal after she'd chased a Xanax with two pints of beer. (Note to impressionable readers: Mixing drugs and alcohol is extremely inadvisable—even for digital robots.)

Again, I tried the "New Words" button. This time, I heard a pathetic yawn followed by a fierce, runaway balloon fart. *What the...?*

On the verge of ripping my head bald, I tried the "Play Again" option. Nope.

I imagined that someone on the other end of this process had turned to her coworker and asked, "Why would a person who's both blind *and* deaf try to buy theater tickets online?"

Having failed to decode every visual and audio hint provided, I clicked on the link of last resort: the "Help" button.

A dropdown box appeared to further obscure the page. "If you are not sure what the words are, either enter your best guess or your mother's middle name because, statistically speaking, both offer equal chances of being incorrect."

Or at least, it might just as well have said that.

Having already tried multiple guesses, I continued

reading. "Click the link labeled 'Vision Impaired' to hear a set of eight digits slurred by an Ambien-laced, slack-jawed, toothless volunteer." Okay, maybe I made up that part about the volunteer. It was likely a union job.

Digits? Had those utterances been *numbers* and not letters? The guidelines had directed me to type in the identified *words*. Sure, vocalized consonants and vowels might sound similar to numeric expressions—when both are *pooted* through a tuba.

The directions provided an explanation for what CAPTCHAs (**C**ompletely **A**utomated **P**ublic **T**uring test to tell **C**omputers and **H**umans **A**part) are and how they're used. "If a correct solution is received, it can be presumed to have been entered by a human."

To further clarify, that's a human who isn't: over age 40, sleep-deprived, memory-impaired, hungover, on antidepressants, or in need of anger management classes. Other exceptions may comprise individuals suffering from impulse control disorders, including, but not limited to, episodes of sudden, unexplained emotional outbursts and unbridled acts of computer vandalism.

According to an expert resource—Wikipedia—people who commonly struggle with visual CAPTCHAs include the partially sighted, colorblind, dyslexic, elderly, and individuals with intellectual disabilities. Seeing as how I must fit into one of those categories, I immediately considered filing for government assistance.

Armed with new information, I circled back to the visual CAPTCHA page and plugged in what I thought matched the inane scrawl on the screen. This time, I added the numbers 6 and 1, which I'd found lurking behind a multi-shaded box adjacent to the garbled letters. I hadn't observed this section earlier, most likely because my eyesight had been diminished by a sudden bout of hypertension.

Instantly, the page changed, and a seating chart appeared. Plenty of tickets remained available for this one-day-only special engagement.

I had zero trouble guessing why.

RULES OF ENRAGEMENT

I'M A STICKLER FOR FOLLOWING the law, but I don't always adhere to rules. (I believe my writing attests to that.) For instance, I have been known, on more than one occasion, to violate the six-garment limit for some store dressing rooms.

What's going to happen if I carry in seven items of apparel? Are the walls so flimsy that they can't support that much weight? Do the store clerks file for Worker's Compensation if they have to reclaim more than six articles from a dressing room?

Once when I tried to sneak in with an extra garment or two, the dressing room gatekeeper stopped me and said, "You'll have to leave one item with me." She wasn't amused when I offered her my shoes.

Some of my favorite discounter's guidelines aggravate me too. During a recent visit, a cashier asked, "Can I see your driver's license?"

"Why?" I'd been frantically searching through my wallet for coupons and had forgotten that along with a hundred dollars' worth of groceries, a few Christmas gifts, and some wrinkle cream, I'd picked up a bottle of wine.

The gal, who looked about 16 years of age, said, "I need to see your birthdate." She stared at me as though she intended to hold my merchandise hostage as long as necessary to enforce compliance.

My driver's license was wedged so tightly into the little plastic holder in my wallet that I couldn't easily pull it free. "Can't I just *tell* you the date?" I asked, irked at being carded by a girl young enough to be my granddaughter.

"No. I have to key in the date, and I'm supposed to *see* the license."

I huffed. "I better get a birthday present from this store."

"Just give her the license," my husband drawled. "What's the big deal?"

He'd never witnessed what it took for me to remove my I.D. from its holder, and he didn't realize that if I handed the cashier my billfold, the thirty coupons I'd wedged in the center would litter the floor. Besides, I was still picking through those coupons trying to see which ones I could use.

Was I just being obstinate? Possibly. But if I'm going to follow rules, I want them to make sense—to me. That checker could have keyed in any date I might have given her, and it wouldn't have mattered. Nobody from the alcohol and firearms department was going to check my birth records against the store's computer. "No, really, touch my neck," I wanted to say. "See? It's not latex. Why do you think I need this Retinol cream?"

Unfortunately, I'm not the only family member who balks at rules. My two sons learned to be nonconformists from early ages. I forgot to tell them that when I said to question everything in life, I didn't mean *my* directives.

"Stop that," I said to my eldest son Ron.

He was sitting across from me in a restaurant booth, unscrewing the caps on the salt and pepper shakers. At 16, he loved to play practical jokes, so I knew what he was doing.

Ron's lips curled into a mischievous grin. "Why?"

"Because the next person will come along and use that salt shaker and ruin their food, and you know it."

He laughed, then picked up a spoon and balanced it upside down on the end of his nose.

I searched my purse for cash so I could pay the bill without a wait. His antics were making my right eye twitch. "Will you act your age?"

He continued with the spoon trick.

I glared at him.

Ron returned a defiant look.

I finished off my soda. "Seriously, you need to quit that now, or I'm going to walk off and leave you here."

Ron removed the spoon, picked up his straw, and inserted the drinking aid into one nostril. "You better not. Trust me. You don't want to do that."

A single mother at that time, I knew I couldn't let this attention-seeking kid get the better of me. I placed a few bills on the table and bolted from the booth. I would ignore my son's clown behaviors and deny him the reaction he was seeking. Maybe then he'd stop embarrassing me in public.

I'd stepped a few feet from the table when I heard someone cry, "Mahhhm, puleeze, don't leh mehh." The plea sounded as though it had come from an afflicted adult.

Hesitantly, I looked over my shoulder.

Shuffling as though he possessed only one normal leg and with an arm curled backward, his hand drawn and gnarled, Ron spastically lurched in my direction. With his other hand, the good one, he reached out to me. "Mahhhm," he again cried. "Don't lea'e mehh!"

I sprinted for the exit, my face hot with shame.

"Mahhhm!" Ron shouted louder.

Please let this floor open and swallow me right now. Behind me, I could hear my insolent son sliding his faked, gimp leg at a faster clip. As I bisected patrons, a man and two women shot me life-threatening glares. I expected someone to karate kick me before I made it to the parking lot.

Safely inside my vehicle, I refused to heed my first thought. It's illegal to abandon your children, even when they provoke you. Though I waited for Ron to rejoin me, I contemplated stowing him in the trunk.

Ron opened the car door.

"What on earth was that?" I demanded.

He climbed inside the vehicle, hee-hawing too hard to respond. When he finally caught his breath, he said, "I *told* you not to leave. You should have listened."

Ryan, my youngest son, must have been taking notes while his brother was growing up. I lost him in a Lowe's home improvement center when he was 15. At the time, my husband and I were deliberating over bathroom fixtures.

"I don't know if that's going to work," I said. "The sink fixtures won't match the shower if we go with that one."

"The sinks are in a separate room," Hubby reminded me.

"True." I considered another manufacturer's product. "What about this one?" I pointed at a boxed showerhead.

He screwed up his face. "Have you seen Ryan?"

I studied the aisle, canted my head, and listened for any noises. In the distance, something buzzed. It sounded like one of those forklifts the store sometimes used indoors. "Nuh-uh. He's around here someplace. He'll find us."

My spouse seemed distracted. Maybe he wanted me to make the final call on the purchase. Still surveying shower fixtures, I heard him say, "Omigod, is that *Ryan*?"

I glanced to my left. Rolling toward us at full power was a store scooter, the kind reserved for those who're too feeble for self-propulsion. Ryan had apparently made a pass through the plumbing department, where he'd nabbed two toilet plungers. He gripped one in each hand, the rubber ends facing toward us, as he jousted with an imaginary knight headed in an opposite direction.

"Ryan!" I yelled. "What are you doing? Those are for *crippled* people."

"Do you see any of 'em in this store?" he asked.

I had to admit I didn't. I struggled to hold a straight face. "How did you learn to operate that thing?"

No one in the family owned a scooter, though I'd been receiving solicitations to buy one by mail.

"I ride them all the time at Walmart. My dad doesn't care," Ryan said, referencing my ex-husband.

"Well, I *do*. So put that back where you found it."

There's a reason why I don't own a dog. I've already failed enough at obedience training.

QUEEN OF THE ROAD

S HE HOPPED A CURB, DROVE over a twenty-foot row of shrubbery, flipped me the middle finger, and screamed something that appeared unloving. I could only see her vile, but oddly humorous, lip movements. Her words remained blissfully inaudible. That is one advantage of owning a decent car stereo.

I sat in my Hyundai, waiting to turn left across a congested street. The woman making an idiot of herself and an ATV of her Tahoe had been parked behind me. She'd grown impatient with my unwillingness to pull forward into oncoming traffic, which could have saved her 30 seconds of wait time. Probably she was in a hurry to get to the day spa, nail salon, or her Pilates class. She didn't seem the type for yoga.

Because I live near Dallas, I've become accustomed to these conditions. I've been honked at for obeying school zones, passed from the wrong lane—as in from the median or outside shoulder—and chased through a parking lot by a couple of angry *Dukes of Hazard*-like guys who weren't savvy enough to comprehend a turn signal. I'd been attempting a right turn as they'd been taking a left, so I had the right-of-way. But right-of-way only counts with drivers who aren't stoned.

The Duke twins were driving a classic muscle car that looked as though it had recently won a mud derby...or maybe been stolen from a pig farmer. The mullet heads gave up their pursuit when they realized I had Bluetooth cellular service and the ability to read their license plate.

Yeah, don't mess with me. I'm armed with intelligence.

Lest you think I'm a terrible driver, let me assure you that is not the case. I've never once invited a wreck or struck anything *unintentionally.* Okay, there was that one time when I pulled into the intersection during an ice storm and someone clipped my car. But I'm from Texas. We're not supposed to know how to drive during a wintery mix. We barely maneuver through rainstorms. Precipitation isn't something we're used to. Road rage, however, is as common as dirt.

According to a survey conducted by AutoVantage, an auto and travel discount provider, the Dallas/Fort Worth region ranks second in the entire U.S. in reported road rage incidents. Only New York has a worse reputation, most likely because of all the taxi drivers. A cabbie's idea of defensive driving is remembering to honk before running a red light.

The AutoVantage survey named DFW the king of tailgating. Even New York didn't top us at bumper-to-bumper motoring. Though Texans share the most expansive state land mass, we're the most resistant when it comes to giving up space between automobiles. It's not that we don't understand a safe stopping distance is one car length for each 10 mph of travel speed. We simply choose to measure that in *Matchbox* terms.

I wasn't surprised by my hometown's driving record. What caught me off guard was a CareerBuilder.com survey that revealed women are more prone to road rage than men. Or perhaps we're more inclined to be honest when surveyed.

If gals really are more apt to lose their emotions behind the wheel, then guys ought to assist with car pool duties. And men should carefully rethink riding our butts.

Reading further, I noted that all of the participants in the CareerBuilder survey were *employed* outside the home. That explained the discrepancy between men and women. Mothers are the ones who're always racing to daycare, trying to get there before closing time, hoping to evade an exorbitant late fine. Who could blame a gal for driving on sidewalks or cutting off other drivers to keep her baby from being ransomed?

My mother, who learned to drive in her early thirties, was a stay-at-home mom and never faced such a proposition, but she spent a lifetime dodging those who did. As a young teen, when I'd ask to go somewhere after 3:00 p.m. on a weekday, Mom would look at the clock and say, "No, we can't go. There's not enough time."

Mom didn't drive during "rush hour," and she rarely went anywhere after dark. So I had no frame of reference for road rage until I earned my own driver's license and began sharing byways with fearless commuters. Then I *knew* why Mom never wanted to drive past three o'clock: too many armed travelers competing for pavement.

During rush hour, which is actually about four

hours long here, the freeways come to a crawl and city streets clog. By the time drivers are halfway home, they're ready to fight the next person who taps his brakes or ignores a This Lane Ends sign. I'm speaking purely from what I've witnessed, of course. I would never start a brawl with another driver, though I'm not above ending one. After all, I'm a woman.

Whether male or female, we Texans long for unimpeded travel. That open-range feeling still resides in our DNA. Instead of herding cattle cross-country, we're now steering cars, and we want those little doggies to get along at a decent speed. If we can't move them fast enough one way, then by golly, we'll cut a new cow path!

That explains why Texas currently holds the country's top speed limit of 85 mph. This speed restriction has been established for State Highway 130, a 41-mile stretch of toll road that bypasses Austin. While many choose to visit that city famous for its capital status, university, and world-class music, others desire to skirt its stifling traffic.

I imagine Highway 130 will greatly reduce road rage because statistics show that angry drivers are often triggered by the act of passing. At 95 mph, the speed at which everyone will be driving if the limit is 85, it'll be next to impossible for one vehicle to ever overtake another.

This new Texas Autobahn will lure Type-A personalities and their heavy feet. Those impatient speeders will be diverted from Interstate 35, which runs parallel to the toll road, out into the vast prairielands. So motorists prone to DWI (Driving

While Infuriated) will be sequestered from folks who've learned to manage their emotions until they get home.

Posting an 85 mph speed limit is more or less a public notice to safe drivers that says, "This road ain't for you." That means all the slowpokes will stay on the interstate, where creeping along at 55 mph isn't likely to get them shot. The rest of us can fly the new toll road into the Wild West, which technically runs south and veers east before intersecting with God knows what.

In a single night, three collisions with wildlife took place on State Highway 130. One deer and two hogs met their makers, and three autos had their shocks thoroughly tested. I read about this road-kill-filled evening in the newspaper, and all I could think was "That's not the best way to handle the state's feral hog problem."

I'm not sure why people need to be driving 85 mph at night unless they're dope smugglers or intent on using their vehicles to catch dinner, in which case this toll road should be their first choice of route.

Apparently, whatever wildlife wanders the range can access Highway 130 for free. And if luck strikes, a driver can pick up a side of pork or venison as he travels. Road warriors can now do what they've always wanted: use their vehicles as weapons. (No hunting license required.) It wouldn't surprise me if the toll road owners upped the fees to profit from the trophy potential.

I find it a bit odd that the state's fastest moving tollway was financed by a firm named SH130 *Concession* Company. When I think of concessions,

DIANA ESTILL

highways don't come to mind. Sporting events do. Yet there's nothing sporting about racing a 300-plus horsepower engine against a single deer or pig. The poor thing may be trying to get hitched, but not to a bumper. Ah, well, better to take your chances sharing a road with wild animals, I suppose, than with a string of puttering drivers. That's especially true if you're female.

Uh oh. Where does the time go? I need to visit Costco, swing by the pharmacy, and pick up something for dinner. I had better skedaddle because it's nearly three o'clock!

104

STUPID ECONOMIC THEORIES

WITH 23 MILLION AMERICANS OUT of work, politicians deriding each other's fiscal policies, and the U.S. Treasury acting like Kinko's, I'm taking responsible action. Yes, that's right. I'm storing cat food and buying men's underwear.

The pet food pretty much speaks for itself. Everyone knows Tuna *Feast* is cheaper than tuna *fish*. But you might wonder about the undershorts, so let me explain.

According to Alan Greenspan (you may recall him as the chief economist prescient enough in 2005 to profess there were no signs of a housing bubble), sales of men's underwear can serve as an economic indicator of our country's financial health.

Men's drawers—the kind they wear, not the ones where they hide their magazines—apparently can support future populations in more ways than one.

Greenspan's underwear theory posits that when times are hard, men are soft. No. Wait. That's not right. He said that during rough times, males buy fewer undergarments. And when the economy is on the verge of a rebound, there's an uptick in the sale of sports briefs and boxer shorts. No mention was made as to where that might lead. I'm guessing to fewer online chats and more suspicions.

Having studied economics for two full semesters, I feel qualified to say that underwear models like Greenspan's—as opposed to Victoria's Secret's—brought us the Great Recession.

If Federal Reserve chairmen have been looking to men's underwear sales to provide hints of economic recovery, they're neither reliable prognosticators nor trustworthy public servants. In fact, they're no different than any other men who suggest the secret to betterment resides in their briefs.

Now, I've known all along that you can get a rise out of a pair of Jockey shorts, but I never realized my spouse's skivvies could lift an entire economy! If there's any merit to this notion, an economic stimulus package could be less effective than my husband's when it comes to moving the GDP (Gross Deceptive Practices) needle.

However, according to recent data, men's underwear sales had been increasing while the economy remained stalled. I tossed this idea to my man to see what explanations he might offer.

"Maybe the economy is so bad that men are crapping their pants, throwing away their underwear, and having to buy more," hubby said. "After a while, you have to do something about those skid marks."

But I saw several more holes in Greenspan's underwear theory.

Maybe it's simply cheaper to buy drawers that were made in Vietnam than it is to launder them in the U.S. Have you seen the prices of detergents lately? Not to mention the cost of electricity to run those newfangled washers and dryers. I could totally justify buying replacement underwear instead of laundering my old ones, especially those with the exhausted elastic and no life left in the crotch. The panties' crotch, I mean.

Perhaps men (and women, too, but evidently we don't count) are too broke to buy food and are therefore eating less. As their weights decline, so do their waistlines. Thus, gentlemen are forced to either lose their shorts or buy new ones. From the looks of the saggy pants I've seen lately, some of both must be going on.

It's also possible that more women are embracing a trend I learned about some time ago. An eccentric relative once told my grandmother that she no longer purchased ladies' underwear. Proudly, my kin displayed the boxer shorts she wore as she explained she saw no need to buy two kinds of undies for the household. One, she said, could work fine for both sexes. Correspondingly, I might add, this family member never bore any children. I imagine her husband couldn't get past his own trunks, so to speak.

Frankly, I question the validity of this whole underwear idea. I doubt men's shorts can tell you anything more than their hygiene habits. But for the sake of science, I'm willing to go with it.

If the Feds need some help devising better economic models, I can think of several. Here are a few:

Gold Party Theory—An inverse relationship exists between the economy and the number of home parties offering attendees a chance to convert gold jewelry to cash.

Walmart Theory—Fewer Walmart store openings in the U.S. suggest an economic upswing is on the way.

Tent Theory—An increase in camping tent sales signals an increase in foreclosures and a decline in GDP. (Note: May also have a dampening effect on the hospitality and cruise industries.)

Roots Theory—A significant rise in the number of women who're displaying a half-inch or more of root color signals an economic recession. (If you don't believe me, poll some hairdressers.)

But this is a serious matter. Our economy is so bad that sleeplessness has become another gauge of fiscal health. One in three Americans report they cannot sleep for worrying about their finances. The other two-thirds can't stay awake on account of depression. I might have guessed at that last part, but...snnnn...grunt, grunt, zzzz...

Excuse me. I nodded off. Where was I?

Oh, yes.

It's time for women everywhere to show solidarity. The country's financial success depends on us!

Ladies are the purveyors of most clothing, including, I suspect, men's underwear. So technically, we're the ones whose purchases are fueling or stalling the economy. We're also in the driver's seat when it comes to buying holiday and birthday gifts. And I don't need to tell you how many of those purchases wind up being functional presents. Show me a married man with a smart wife, and I'll show you a guy whose holidays include Hanes.

What I'm saying here is that economists really

ought to think twice before proffering stupid economic concepts that dismiss women's contributions. Otherwise, we might all stop buying men's undies and trigger the next recession.

BERRY FALSE ADVERTISING

H AVING SUCCUMBED TO THE IDEA that I needed a new lip color, I accidentally purchased a product designed to enhance my pucker. Never would I have knowingly bought such a lipstick. But I had failed to take my reading glasses shopping. So I'm fortunate that discount stores don't display Bengay on the same aisle with cosmetics.

On the lipstick container, I could barely make out the letter "X," which I thought might be some kind of color rating. It wasn't until I returned home with the purchase and put on my spectacles that I read the words, "Berry Desirable."

Oh, *yeah.* I could practically hear Marvin Gaye singing.

I peeled open the lipstick and sampled the shade that suggested it would turn me into a siren—or as it turned out, simply make me sound like one.

"Yow-ow-ee! What's in this stuff?"

See, that's the danger of spending too much time alone in front of a mirror. You start asking questions to the ethers and *expecting* to hear voices. I half presumed an invisible Bryan Williams would intone, "The answer is: Vitamin E, propylparaben, red dye number six, Ethylbarbitrol, LucyRicardosol, and active ingredient, one percent Angelina Jolie DNA solution."

Truth be told, I've no idea what was in that lipstick because I've long since disposed of it. Suffice it to say, Berry Desirable would have been more accurately labeled Berry Uncomfortable.

I was about to dab my lips with a tissue when my husband entered the bathroom and found me grimacing before the mirror. "What's wrong?" he asked.

"This lipstick I bought is burning my lips."

He leaned toward me and puckered his kisser. "Let's see what it does to mine."

I kissed him, making sure to smear as much rose-colored stain on his lips as possible.

"It tingles," he confirmed. "What's it *supposed* to do?"

"It's one of those lip-plumping kinds." I sighed. "I accidentally bought the wrong one."

His eyes lit up. "What if it makes *my* lips plump?"

I chuckled. "It won't make you look like Mick Jagger. But it might make you jump like him."

Behind the tube's "Peel for caution" indicator, hid this warning: "Discontinue if you experience excessive discomfort."

What did the manufacturer mean by *excessive* discomfort? Was mild to moderate discomfort expected? Come to think of it, maybe I *had* confused the lipstick with a sports cream.

I don't know why I need to have plumper lips, anyway. Why must I look like a blowfish to be attractive to the opposite sex? Oh, hold on. I just reread that last question and think I found my answer.

But seriously, how much pain must I endure

and money must I spend to achieve a sexy, pouty mouth? (No, not a potty mouth. There's no effort involved in that.)

Men don't worry about how their lips look. Some of them, and I won't name any names here, don't even *have* lips. That's why they grow mustaches. I tried that once, but it looked horribly unflattering on me.

If all the marketing hype I read is correct, I need to sell at least 100,000 books per year to remain attractive to my guy. I say this because staying pretty is a pricey proposition these days. In addition to lip-plumping lipstick, to keep my allure, I need to purchase—quite possibly in bulk supply—the following items:

- Non-clumping mascara
- Under-eye brightener cream
- Perfume
- Skinny jeans (to make me "look thinner")
- Triple-power, anti-aging face cream (which is sure to be followed by quadruple power within six months, forcing me to upgrade)
- Skin-glowing foundation (Am I supposed to be a lady or a lantern?)
- Volumizing, vitamin-infused shampoo
- Hair straightening potions
- Hydrating facial masks
- Rejuvenating facial cleansers
- Gel manicure/pedicure products
- Laser hair removal
- Shapewear (to smooth my bulges)
- Sunless tanning lotion

This list of feminine necessities (and many more) can be verified by perusing the first half of any women's magazine. The second half of those rags reveals something altogether different. Gals seldom read that far, most likely because they've grown too despondent.

This body image brainwashing has been unequally dispensed between the sexes. Men aren't inundated with marketing messages that damage their self-esteem, question their appeal to women, or suggest they might be happier as a hermit. As long as they own a pickup truck, use a sports stick deodorant, and "can be ready when the time is right," they're done. But most guys think *any* time is the right time. So I suppose they have to be perpetually prepared, which, come to think of it, is what they expect of women.

Where is a female's equivalent for Cialis? When I want to insure arousal, I can't simply take a pill. I have to swallow a truffle. And that just plays hell with my weight, which leaves me feeling unmotivated. Who needs sex when there are gourmet chocolates?

If the world was fair, meaning if women were in charge of everything, guys would find ads for the following products in their sports publications:

- Facial creams to tighten sagging chin lines
- Special lotions to thicken chest hair
- Wonderjock underwear (Google it.)
- Naughty nightwear to help them feel sexy
- Laser ear and nose hair removal
- Testes augmentation surgery
- Shoes that permanently ruin feet yet make them

look taller
- Special occasion socks
- Wrinkle-erasing aftershave
- Eye drops that give them that steely-eyed, do-me gaze

To really balance the scales, men's magazines should include articles on subjects like, "Three Positions to Drive Your Woman Wild!" and "Having it All: How to Balance Family, Career, Carpool, Fitness, In-laws, Pets, and Household Cleaning and Still Make Time for Cuddling." And these magazines would picture athletes on their covers, men posed in seductive positions. The stars would be baring their abs, and their images would be airbrushed to make them look better than a romance cover model.

If such fantasies ever come true, I know exactly what I'll do when I see one of those magazines. I'll lift the journal, gawk at the cover, and say to my spouse, "Wow! *He* sure looks *good* for fifty!"

Ah, for now, I'm simply going to focus on having luscious lips without looking as if I'm having a peanut allergy attack.

CYLINDER FETISH

MY LOVE AFFAIR WITH CYLINDERS started when I was a teen. Straight hair was the rage during the 1960s, thanks to icons like Cher. Long, board-flat tresses, parted down the middle, with or without bangs, became the desire of most every girl under age 20. But that look was almost impossible to achieve for those like me who had thick, curly hair that would frizz when anyone sneezed. That's why I became obsessed with cans.

"Don't throw that away!" I begged every time I saw my mom ditching what had previously stored frozen orange juice. She would look at me as if I'd just suggested we boil a possum for dinner, though she usually obliged my requests.

With an electric opener, I'd remove the remaining end from the can and store the metal tube away for future use. The bigger the can, the better and straighter my hair would turn out. I'd pull my thick wet strands into a tight ponytail on top my head (*I Dream of Jeannie* style) and then roll the ponytail onto the modified container. Oversized bobby pins secured the metal curler in place. This is how I slept most nights, which might explain why I have not yet needed a brow lift.

Mornings when I awoke and brushed out my mane,

a slight hair crimp that began at my temples and circled the back of my head remained. The rubber band I used to hold my ponytail in place caused this unwanted wave. To remove that last ripple, I'd cinch my hair tight at the nape for an hour before school. This, of course, caused a new wave to form at neck level. So I would tug at my locks as I rode the school bus, hoping to remove all traces of hair memory. The whole ordeal was so masochistic that I feared I might one day become a "cutter."

Soon I graduated from juice to vegetable cans because they offered greater diameter. Over time, my hair outgrew canned corn. That's when I moved on to oatmeal cartons. The boxes kept getting soggy and wilting during the night, so that idea had to be scrapped. Not only did the hot breakfast cereal containers work poorly, but the wait for oatmeal cartons to empty flat surpassed my patience.

No longer a desperate teen, I thought I'd outgrown my fascination with cylinder-shaped objects. Well, okay, at least *most* of them. But today, while standing in my favorite discounter's hair care aisle, I felt a rush when I glimpsed a curling iron of grand magnitude.

I already owned a curling iron hefty enough to make my husband jealous. But the instrument hanging at eye-level exceeded my dreams! Its barrel was as big as the business end of a baseball bat. I could really straighten some tresses with that hair buddy! Of course, if I wasn't careful, I could also scald half my face.

My first accident occurred before I'd even opened the instrument. I gouged myself while freeing the unit from its clamshell package. So essentially, I became a cutter after all.

Inside the container, I found a folded sheet of paper with the words "Save these instructions" in bold print.

How much guidance would I need to push the "on" button, wait for the iron to heat, and sear my forehead? I'd done that a thousand times already. It would require more than instructions to give me better hand-to-head coordination. But I decided to take a peek anyway. Maybe there was more to be concerned about than facial burns.

The warnings stated, "Do not use an appliance *whose* cord has become twisted." Did this curling iron possess human qualities? Besides getting hot and being rather, uh, well-endowed, that is. Why use the word "whose" to refer to an inanimate object?

Amused, I continued reading. Among the curling iron's critical instructions were such pearls of wisdom as "Barrel remains *hot* when in use." I was advised also never to use the product near water.

"Near" water? How close is "near?" Would standing two feet from the bathroom sink be too close? Only if the sink is filled, right? But what if there were *drops* of water in the bottom of the bowl? Then should I towel dry the sink, first? Wait a minute. What constitutes "water?" I mean, does saliva count?

My runaway worries didn't stop there.

"Do not use outdoors or operate where aerosol products are being used." Ignoring the obvious word repetition, I questioned who would want to engage a curling iron outdoors. However, I considered the aerosol reference might have some validity. If I used the device in the bathroom, I'd be standing in the same room where I often employ air fresheners and hairspray. If I couldn't engage the curling iron in my bathroom or outdoors, maybe the gadget had been designed for bedroom use. As tempting as that line is, I'm not going *there*.

The funniest directive said, and I am not making this up, "Never drop or insert *any* object into *any* opening." I'm pretty sure most men would take exception to that. The curling iron didn't come with any attachments, and it had no openings, so unless the manufacturer was hoping to include birth control advice with its product usage instructions, I'm not sure what purpose that statement served.

Finally, the warnings included this recommendation: "Do not use while sleeping." I'm thinking this must have been speaking to Ambien users. Who else would fix their hair during sleep? Somewhere out there in Product Liability Land, attorneys are being paid big money to protect their clients against these kinds of remote risks. Perhaps lawyers might also like to include a few more cautionary statements, such as:

- Do not use after drinking three or more alcoholic beverages.
- Do not use while sedated or taking recreational drugs.
- Never use while texting, driving, or piloting aircraft.
- Do not use during a hurricane, tornado, or earthquake.
- Avoid use if you are unable to discern hot from cold or to feel pain.
- Not intended for cooking, soldering, or

cattle branding.

Despite all the silly instructions, I operated my new curling iron while standing in front of the sink in my bathroom. Electrocution seemed about as likely as getting zapped by lightning. My hair came out so straight that I wondered what might happen if I found an iron with an even larger barrel. Now if only I could find a device the size of an oatmeal can...

BELLY DANCER

AFTER TWENTY YEARS OF MARRIAGE, my husband and I have few surprises to offer each other. As Valentine's Day approached, I considered what I might do to spice up the evening—other than tie love notes to the TV controller.

That's why I secretly ordered an instructional DVD that promised to turn me into a seductress. The sales blurb stated the featured belly dance routines were suitable for "all body types." By this, the writer apparently meant all *athletic* body types. I pulled a hamstring during my first shimmy.

To help me get "into" my new role, I purchased, online, a belly dance skirt—one embellished with dime-sized coins that clinked together so that it sounded like I'd hit a slot machine jackpot every time I shook my hips. This too was sold as a "one size fits all" item. The diaphanous black mini-skirt had been designed to tie at the bikini-line, or where my bikini-line used to be. I made a sash, tightening the strings as much as possible, and still the sides gapped apart four inches. Perhaps someone should consider making these garments to fit *American* women.

Undeterred, I hid my DVD and undersized costume and waited until Hubby went to work before I watched the video. This instructional movie had to be audited before I would commit to exerting any physical effort. The teacher, who looked like a centerfold model, began by discussing the art of belly dance. She made the movements appear simple to copy—for anyone over 5' 11" with long limbs and a graceful carriage. I, however, happen to be under 5' 3" and have a figure more akin to a Sumo wrestler than a supermodel.

Nonetheless, I cinched my noisy skirt and pretended to be Shakira. But every time I bounced my hips I sounded like a washing machine full of pennies. On the spin cycle.

The video separated dance movements into categories: arms, hips, and simple routines. I decided to work on getting down the arm motions first. Then I'd return to my larger muscle groups, which seemed to have temporarily confused belly dancing with disco.

To make sure I practiced good form, I moved my laptop computer (in which I'd inserted the DVD) onto my bathroom counter. By standing in front of the counter mirror, I could simultaneously watch myself and view the instructor. Observing my reflection, I discovered the unflattering effects of having two small hams swinging from where my triceps should have been.

Initially, I'd put on a sports bra to help me see my stomach muscles—or the space where my abs used to reside. But once I witnessed how much less attractive a belly roll can be when it's joined by cellulite, I moved my attention upward.

The undulating shoulder movements I attempted

were overshadowed by the draping wads of arm fat that swung in counter-time to the music beat. My snake-like arm motions looked as though they'd been made by a pair of boa constrictors—after they'd each swallowed a rabbit. Definitely not the image I was aiming to achieve.

Searching my closet, I found a long-sleeve, black, stretch-fit shirt to stop, or at least hide, my arm flaps. Wearing that and the black Lycra pants with the belly dance skirt tied around my hips, I looked like an Egyptian mime.

Yes, I could definitely see how this might surprise my spouse. Just not in the way I'd originally hoped.

Belly dancers keep their arms extended throughout their routines. This, I soon learned, looks much easier than it actually is. To best describe the muscle stress that five minutes of belly dancing can deliver, imagine being tied for that long by both wrists to two bedposts. Not that I'd know what that feels like. I'm just saying...

I couldn't make it through the ten-minute upper body instructional without taking breaks to relax my arms. Any routine I performed for Hubby would need to be short-lived. I'd previously planned as much anyway, though for much more favorable reasons.

Moving on to the hip movement instructions, I expected to do better. After all, I did live through the '70s. Shaking my booty was something I'd perfected long ago. Only now, I had more mass to set in motion...and fewer reasons to do so. Today, when I wiggle my behind, the attention I attract comes mainly from fitness trainers and diet counselors.

Shimmying came easily to me. At least, *starting* the quivering action was relatively simple.

Stopping it was another matter.

My torso and upper limbs didn't understand they were supposed to move independent of my hips. The brain sent my upper body the same signals it gave my lower half. My shoulders shuddered, my boobs shook, and my head bobbled despite my best attempts to hold those parts still. With my entire body convulsing, I looked as if I might be doing an impression of Joe Cocker.

Joining the cast of *Riverdance* would likely be out of question for me, too. Not that my husband would be turned on by Irish folk-dancing. As far as I know, that only works for men who're much older.

By the time I'd made it through half the video, I'd grown too fatigued to finish. But Valentine's Day remained nearly two weeks away, so I expected that would allow me sufficient time to perfect my dancing skills.

Each day, while my spouse was at work, I practiced belly dancing. However, I gained only a modest amount of upper body strength and rhythmic coordination. I truly hoped I could get the hang of it well enough to perform an abbreviated dance of some sort. I questioned whether men really care how much of a woman's body shimmies *together*. Once a gal's breasts engage motion, I imagine all other parts of her anatomy become invisible.

After I'd followed along through the first full routine, I could barely lift a fork without hurting. I hadn't ached that much since I'd last tried to do a chin-up—without a stepstool. The belly dance video hadn't turned me into a siren, but more like a screaming alarm. I whined every time I lifted my blow-dryer. This was supposed to be fun, not painful. If I had wanted to feel like that, I'd have bought a Pilates video!

—————◦⟋⟋◦—————

As Valentine's Day grew nearer, I wondered if I'd ever really do a belly dance for anyone besides my cat. Even she, by the way, couldn't stay awake through my trial performances.

In early February, our city experienced the worst arctic storm in fifteen years. Eight inches of snow and ice blanketed the roads, making the freeways impassable, which meant my husband had to work from home.

I hid my belly dance video and shimmy skirt, knowing I couldn't practice until the streets thawed. At least my muscles could recover, and for a few days, I could quit eating with plastic utensils. Yet no sooner had the temperatures climbed above the freeze mark than they plummeted again. A second round of snow left Hubby home for another full day, assuring I'd never learn my routine in time for Valentine's Day.

February fourteenth arrived without precipitation, so I drug out my belly dance attire and attempted to get through a short routine. So much time had elapsed between practices that it felt as though I was starting over from the beginning. With any luck, my man would forget I'd promised him a "surprise" that evening. Short of a miracle, I wasn't going to pull off my plan. At least, not before summer—and then I would need to rethink my whole outfit.

When hubby came home from work, I said, "How

about staying home tonight? We can just eat here, *in front of the television.*"

He never asked me about the surprise I'd mentioned, probably because all he heard was the word "television." Maybe I should have skipped the whole dance idea and taken a shortcut. I could have simply slipped my belly dance DVD into the player and achieved a more desirable effect.

But ever the optimist, I'm still hoping to one day perform a belly dance for my spouse—possibly on his birthday. I'm just not going to get overambitious and specify what year.

SURPRISE MAKEOVER

E VERY TIME I LOOK IN the mirror, I see my mother's neck.

Friends, I'm here to tell you that you can hide from your HOA, skip Sunday services, dodge the neighbors, and ignore your spouse, but you cannot escape family genetics. If your parents were screamers, you'll probably be one too. And if your mom had three chins, you might as well plan on forgoing turtlenecks.

My mother passed along many good physical qualities, including shapely legs and long fingers with which to play the piano. She mastered that instrument, though I chose to become proficient at a more portable and less challenging keyboard: the one on my computer.

Along with the positive traits I inherited from Mom, I collected some less desirable ones. For example, my coarse hair, responsible for destroying more than twenty blow dryers, twelve curling irons, and six stylists' careers, can be directly linked to my mother's tresses. It can also be tied to two bad perms and enough bleach to fill a Jacuzzi, but Mom gets most the blame.

The breadth of my hips and lengths of my arms are noticeably the same as my mother's. And the wattle that now sags beneath what's left of my chin looks an awful lot like ones on the woman who birthed me.

But I didn't get all of my mother's physical attributes. When it comes to breasts, I was fortunate enough to receive my dad's.

I'm not saying my mother was totally flat-chested. In her younger years, she was thin and correspondingly small-busted. After having four children, she gained some girth and curves. But as she advanced into her so-called golden years, whatever she'd acquired in the boob department disappeared along with her use for politicians, fancy restaurants, and underwear.

"I'm not wearing a bra," Mom boldly announced during one of her last visits with me. "They're too uncomfortable."

Most women her age had discarded their brassieres in the '70s. But Mom had waited until she was in *her* seventies to let go of hers.

"That's all right," I said. "It's not even noticeable." As soon as I let that slip, I realized she might misconstrue my words. She'd always been sensitive about her figure. I didn't want to add to any insecurity she might still harbor.

"You can have the ones I bought at the Dollar Store," she continued, never acknowledging my response. "I got stuck in one of them darn things and couldn't get it off."

She'd purchased two sports bras, the type that have to be pulled over the head, the kind that even I can't put on or take off without having the holster roll up under my armpits. Those stretchy, python-like boob binders always made me writhe like a performer for Cirque du Soleil. These were not the best undergarment selections for a senior citizen.

The truth was Mom didn't have anything but two tortillas with a pat of butter left where her breasts used to reside. There was no impropriety involved in her missing underwear. Few men were sneaking peeks through the banded-bottom blouses of the elderly. And if I was wrong about that, I didn't want to know it.

Mom had always wrestled with her body image. While she never gave a moment's thought to breast augmentation, she obsessed over her stomach paunch and neck goiter.

"I bought a new machine for my abs from the Home Shopping Club," she announced by phone, less than a year after she'd suffered a heart attack.

"Did your doctor say you could use it?" I asked.

"No! He doesn't know I ordered it."

And that's how it was with Mom. She did what she wanted. Despite her congestive heart failure, she refused to give up on making her belly flatter or her chin visible, even if it netted her nothing more than a decent obit image.

When I saw Mom's online pictures, I noted she looked different. I couldn't quite identify what she'd done to make herself appear younger, but I knew it had nothing to do with abdominal crunches. Maybe her webcam had been tilted at a flattering angle, I decided.

When I visited her in Florida, she divulged her camera secret.

"I hate the way my neck is beginning to sag,"

I confessed to Mom. We were sitting outdoors on her bench swing, ruminating about the crimes of aging. "And how come you never told me to expect chin hair?"

Mom chuckled. "You got chin hair?"

"Yeah! And I never once heard you say a word about anything like that. Why do I have it and you don't?"

Mom laughed harder. "I don't have any because I *shave* mine." She was on the verge of a cackling fit. "If you won't *write* about it, I'll show you my cure for a double-chin." She gave me a look that warned she was serious about not reporting whatever she was about to reveal. "I'll go get it." She stood and then retreated inside.

Now, in fairness, I didn't make her any promises, and Mom is no longer where she can read my books, as far as I know. So I didn't lie to her. Besides, having known me for over fifty years, she surely understood not to trust me with anything this strange.

Mom returned to the swing, carrying something inside one balled fist. She sat down next to me, canted her body toward me, and said, "When I'm online and I don't want people to see my big ol' neck, I just do this."

She slipped a six-inch, flesh-toned rubber band under her chin, looped it behind her ears, and threaded it through her hair. "Instant facelift!"

Knowing how Mom felt about her features, I worried about her final appearance. When she passed away, her roots were showing, her nails hadn't been tended, and her body had been ravaged by cancer. The silly things she'd spent a lifetime trying to improve were no longer a concern. Cancer had stolen all the fat from her body. There is nothing funny about that.

I stood over Mom's casket before anyone else arrived for the viewing. She looked beautiful, prettier than she'd been in years. Her hair had been dyed, her nails trimmed and painted, and her face no longer told the story of her final months of physical torment. I double-checked her for whiskers to be sure there were none. That's what good daughters do. I'm telling you now, when I kick the bucket, my girls better be right there with a Norelco and some brow wax.

Mom wore the lavender dress she'd laid out one week before her death, which as it turned out, had been the sum total of her funeral planning. She hadn't been ready to leave, I know, because she'd forgotten to tell me where she kept that rubber band.

Despite the undertaker's excellent work, something was off about the way Mom looked. She didn't seem natural somehow.

"Does she look normal to you?" I asked my husband.

"Define normal," he replied. "If you mean normal for a dead person who's been embalmed, sure."

Mom's hospice nurse arrived and gave me a hug. Together, we paid our respects. "Something doesn't seem right," I said.

The nurse tilted her head, studied my mother's midsection, and offered nothing.

I followed her gaze. "Ohmigoodness! She has BOOBS!"

The hospice worker snickered and then looked at me apologetically. "I didn't want to say anything. But I noticed it right away."

Evidently, the mortician had tried to improve Mom's appearance to the fullest extent. He'd replaced her bra and even added a little, no, a bunch...I'm talking at least a C cup here, of padding to go with it. Mom looked as though she had implants. In seventy-nine years of life, the woman had never had a breast job, yet her bust had been given a postmortem makeover.

I can't be sure, but I don't think Mom would have disapproved.

THE LAST COOKIE

G ENERALLY SPEAKING, I'M AN OPTIMIST. I believe that, in the end, good triumphs over evil— though the wait can be hell. The sixty pounds I set out to lose this year really can be shed without resorting to diet drugs, a personal trainer, or duct tape, and the people I'll meet in heaven won't include my ex-husbands. (Yes, that was plural because I'm a slow learner.)

But when the U.S. government issued a statement promising the world would *not* end on December 21, 2012, as some people believe the Mayan calendar predicted, an internal alarm sounded. How could the same folks who robbed the Social Security Trust Fund offer assurances about our planet's safety? They can't even accurately estimate next year's federal budget.

Being the positive-thinking person I *try* to be, I decided not to worry about the Mayan calendar's precision. Instead, I scheduled a party for December 21. I had already wanted to host a holiday gathering. And if the world *was* going to end on that date, I might never have a funeral, but I didn't want to be cheated out of a decent wake.

As I penned the party food list, I made sure to include plenty of cookies. Should that event include my last meal, I wanted to go out with one last guilty look on my face and telltale sugar residue dusting my lips. Oh, yes, and maybe a rivulet of Merlot snaking down my chin.

Ideally, my final cookie would be red velvet flavored because those are among my favorites. The possibility of impending death would negate all concerns about calories, carbs, or Red Dye #40. And there'd be no need to fret over pesky carpet stains or leftovers. When I considered the catastrophic ending forecasted, I had to admit a date-certain death could offer benefits. But the trade-offs didn't seem all that appealing.

Because I believed global destruction remained as uncertain as Christina Aguilera's natural hair color, I was unwilling to bake toward that outcome. Thus, I decided to stick with basic sugar cookies sprinkled with sugar crystals. As my grandmother used to say, "You can't ever have too much sweetness." Unless, of course, you are a diabetic or that Honey Boo Boo Child, and then I think we can all agree you need to rein it in.

As an experiment, I decided to make a dozen cookies and decorate them with two different toppings. That would help me decide which coatings tasted best and how far in advance I could make these festive deserts and expect them to remain reasonably fresh.

By "reasonably," I mean the cookies had to be soft enough for guests to chew without chipping any veneers. All I wanted those treats to break was an acquaintance's I'm-skinnier-than-you'll-ever-be attitude.

THIS CAN'T BE NORMAL

You know, every party has that one gal who hovers over the raw veggie tray as if cruciferous foods offer her insurance against looking like the rest of us. Through sheer scientific observation, I can attest that if there's ever a global catastrophe, that bitch is bound to die first.

———&

After my sugar cookie trial run had been completed, I nibbled a morsel with cinnamon sprinkles and compared it to one I'd sanded with red sugar crystals. The Christmas-colored one was superior in both taste and visual appeal. So I devoured another scrumptious disc before locking away the rest inside a plastic container—the clear kind that I could see through, which allowed for easy access and close inspection of the specimens at various intervals.

I intended to sample one cookie each day until the treats no longer met my quality standards. At that point, I'd know how far in advance I could bake the holiday party cookies—and how truthful Hubby had been when he said those indulgences held zero appeal. Right off, he'd snared a cookie with his fingers and pronounced, "They're okay. But they're not chocolate chip."

Well, had they been chocolate chip, I would have already known how far ahead of the event I could risk baking them. Tollhouse treats don't hang around long enough in my kitchen to grow stale. They've been known to disappear during a single TV episode.

Later that evening, I decided a few hours might make a difference in the way a cookie tastes, so I *evaluated* another one.

Still just as good as the first...and second...and third I'd previously sampled.

Now only seven specimens remained to examine over the next several days—provided my restraint stretched that far.

On the second day, the cookie I consumed for breakfast had already lost some of its freshness. However, it remained a tasty, if nutrient-free, food selection. I rationalized that the vanilla flavoring in the cookie dough had come from a bean which had grown on a tree, and sugar comes from cane stalk. So theoretically, my morning entrée was no less wholesome or odd a choice than a scone, which is a pastry so dry that it should be renamed "stone." But I've digressed.

By lunchtime, I'd made another practice run at the cookies. With authority, I can say that twenty-four to thirty-six hours beyond bake time made little difference in the texture of those delectable gems. I could make the cookies at least two days before the party, and no one would notice the difference. Except maybe that lady who thinks she's Paula Deen. And nothing that originated from my kitchen would suit her, anyhow. She was the reason why I'd already crossed "raw veggie tray" off my party food list.

Fearing I might be an inadequate social host, I scarfed down two more cookies.

My subconscious mind whispered, "If you'll just hurry up and eat them all, you'll no longer be tempted." Each nibble seemed better than the last, but the insulin spike I experienced might have unduly influenced my opinion.

Unfortunately, I'm unable to confirm an outcome

for Day Three because I consumed all of my test subjects within forty-eight hours. Also, I gained another pound. But as it turned out, that wasn't the end of the world. It was just my last cookie experiment.

RESEARCH CONCLUSIONS:

- Cookie research may produce undesired symptoms for dieters.
- Paula Deen wannabes are better party caterers than guests.
- The Mayan calendar didn't end in 2012. The Discovery Channel simply needed a ratings boost.
- Sometimes, the government gets lucky.
- In the event of a global cataclysm, my mortality rate should be slightly better than average.

LEAVING HUBERT

I ONCE HAD A NEXT-DOOR NEIGHBOR—I'LL call him Hubert—who refused to ever trim his trees. Though he maintained a vigil over our home for evidence of anything in need of attention, he neglected his own property. Hubert was the kind of guy who would knock on your door during dinnertime just to tell you something about your house or lawn that irked him. Having the Estills for neighbors left him perpetually annoyed. But that feeling was mutual.

Often when I saw Hubert outdoors, I asked him to please cut back the thirty-foot Bradford pear tree that grew from his side of our shared property line. The tree's trunk stood two inches inside Hubert's yard, but the branches knew no boundaries. Tree limbs shaded our side yard so heavily that even weeds could not survive.

One night, I answered a knock at the front door.

Hubert stood on our porch. "Did you know you have a gutter pulling loose on the side of your house?"

I folded my arms across my chest. "Oh, really?"

"Yeah, the nails are pulling loose, and it's kind of hanging," he said, as if he might be fulfilling some kind of HOA duties.

"Gee, maybe that's because *your* tree has been scraping against that gutter for the past two years,

Hubert. Why don't you do me a big favor and trim it…before I do it myself?"

Backing away slowly, he chuckled. "You wouldn't do that."

I grinned like a psycho. "Yes. I would."

Hubert gave me a nervous glance as he walked toward his home.

Soon after that terse discussion, Hubert's house underwent foundation repairs. At the advice of an engineer, Hubert had a "root barrier" installed. This meant that his pear tree's life-support system had been severed on one side. And that caused the tree to lean even more toward our rooftop, giving me yet another reason to glare every time I looked at Hubert's butt crack as he fiddled in his flowerbeds.

One Saturday afternoon, I observed Hubert's family depart in their minivan. "Quick," I said to my husband, "next week is bulk trash week. Let's go trim Hubert's tree."

Hubby's eyes sparked. "Are they gone?"

"Yes, and it looked like they were heading off somewhere for the day."

"I'll help," our youngest son, Ryan, said. Our children knew of our continuing saga with Hubert.

"We can't sell this house without grass in the side yard," I rationalized. "And he's never going to trim that tree. There's nothing left to do but hack that sucker."

Normally, my bunch is opposed to active labor. But this time was different. This wasn't about tree trimming. It was about retribution! For years, we'd asked, first politely, then earnestly, and then pleadingly, that Hubert perform his own botanic amputations.

Each time we inquired about tree trimming, Hubert stared at his tree and smugly offered, "I like the fullness."

So the Estills were on a mission to correct what Hubert had flatly refused to fix.

Despite my love of trees and a desire to preserve their integrity, I viewed Hubert's encroaching Bradford as a combatant. It was a source of destruction to our roof and lawn and a constant reminder of his obstinacy. We hated that tree almost as much as we detested Hubert's flatulence.

Hubert regularly stood on the sidewalk in front of our homes, conversing with us about how he thought we should poison the weeds growing in the sidewalk joints or seal the flashing around our attic vent or making some other such observation, and he'd fart the entire time. He was the only person I knew who could talk and toot without skipping a beat. Not only would he pollute the air around us as he critically evaluated our home maintenance skills, but he'd pretend not to notice the tuba notes escaping from his rump.

We didn't like Hubert or his encroaching tree. In fact, to escape him we were willing to do most anything—including relocate.

"What do you think he'll say when he sees this?" Hubby chopped off a six-foot branch and was assessing the damage. "It looks awful."

"I don't care what he says. He's had this coming for a long time." I studied the lopsided tree, which looked like a tornado survivor. "If he wanted pretty, then he should have done this himself."

Ryan helped me drag the branch to the street,

where we shoved it onto what could easily have been the makings for a suburban bonfire. The stack of limbs had grown to a massive pile about five feet high and two car lengths wide. Hiding the evidence was not an option. We might just as well have hung a sign on our front door that said, "We Did It!" But I wasn't afraid of the outcome. After all, we were planning to move.

The sun was about to set when Ryan yelled, "Here they come!"

Hubert's minivan pulled into view. There was no time to do anything but grab our tools and disappear. I darted for the safety of our garage. Hubby slipped in quickly behind me, and Ryan followed on his heels. I hit the button to close our electric garage door and then let out a guffaw.

"Did you see the looks on their faces?" Ryan asked.

"No," my tree murderer replied. "I made a point not to look at them."

I wanted all the details so I could further relish our victory. "Why? What did they look like?"

"The mom was pointing, and she had her mouth open. Then Hubert stopped his van in the driveway and just stared at the tree." Ryan giggled. "And then all the kids started looking too."

"I'll handle it if he comes over here," Hubby said, all John Wayne-like.

But as it turned out, when Hubert knocked on our door that night, I was the one who answered.

"Uh, I...uh, I see you trimmed my tree." Hubert pointed to the bunker size bunch of branches covering our sidewalk.

"Sure did." I waited for him to make his next move.

"What do I owe you?"

I detected a sarcastic tone. If he'd come looking for a fight, I was ready for him. "Nothing. Three years of grief seemed like it ought to be enough," I replied.

If Hubert had come to tell us off, he decided better of it. He spun on one heel and went back to his house.

The day before we were supposed to close on the sale of our house, my husband received a phone call from the buyer. We had already moved to our new home and were enjoying Hubert-free living.

"I just called to tell you that a tree fell on the roof of your house," the prospective new owner said.

Hubert's now not-so-full Bradford pear tree had snapped at the base and collapsed atop our soon-to-be-sold home. We'd rid ourselves of Hubert, but not his karma.

After Hubby hung up the phone I said, "Ohmigod, do they still want to close tomorrow?"

"Yes, they do." My landscape perpetrator snickered. "And you know what that means?"

"We have to pay for roof damage?"

"No. It means they've met Hubert, and they *still* want the house!"

One year later, the new owners sold the home and relocated to another city. They claim the move was prompted by a job transfer.

But we know better.

ACKNOWLEDGEMENTS

This is where I'm supposed to mention all those who helped make this book possible. So, first, let me thank American Airlines. Without their assistance, I might still be stuck in Barbados, staggering from too much rum-laced pineapple juice.

I must also express my gratitude to my husband, Jim, who allows me to expose his private life to readers and is secure enough to travel this comedic journey with me. Without his love and friendship, my life would be much less full and amusing.

I'd be remiss if I didn't give credit to Mom and Dad, the parents who bore me and who, thank goodness, either can't or won't ever read what I've written. Don't worry, Dad. You aren't missing anything because this book offers no educational value whatsoever.

My family continues to be my best source of writing material, and I thank each and every member for his or her contributions—however unknowingly those may have been conveyed. I'll pay you all back for that...someday. Really. I just hope you won't return the favor.

Lynn McNamee must be recognized for her longsuffering hours spent editing this book. You are my favorite taskmaster, a diligent professional, and a tireless supporter. You deserve kudos for making me a better writer.

And finally, I must acknowledge Streetlight Graphics for their excellent work on cover design and formatting.

ABOUT THE AUTHOR

Diana Estill is the author of four humor books, one novel, and a collection of short stories. She lives in Texas with her husband, whom she regrets may never see her belly dance.

OTHER BOOKS BY DIANA ESTILL

When Horses Had Wings (a novel)

Crap Chronicles (a collection of short stories)

Stilettos No More

Deedee Divine's Totally Skewed Guide to Life

Driving on the Wrong Side of the Road

www.ingramcontent.com/pod-product-compliance
Lightning Source LLC
Chambersburg PA
CBHW031319040426
42443CB00005B/142